WRITERS AND THI

ISOBEL ARMSTR
General Edit

BRYAN LOUGH:
Advisory Edit

VLADIMIR NABOKOV

VLADIMIR NABOKOV

Photograph by Maclean Dameron of Nabokov in Ithaca, 1957 with his novel *Pnin*, for which he had just received a National Book Award nomination. *By courtesy of the Division of Rare and Manuscript Collections, Carl A. Kroch Library, Cornell University.*

VLADIMIR NABOKOV

NEIL CORNWELL

© Copyright 1999 by Neil Cornwell

First published in 1999 by Northcote House Publishers Ltd, Plymbridge House, Estover Road, Plymouth PL6 7PY, United Kingdom.
Tel: +44 (01752) 202368 Fax: +44 (01752) 202330.

British Library Cataloguing-in-Publication Data
A catalogue record for this book is available from the British Library

ISBN 0-7463-0868-X

Typeset by PDQ Typesetting, Newcastle-under-Lyme
Printed and bound in the United Kingdom

Contents

Biographical Outline

Dates before the arrival of the Nabokov family in London (May 1919) are given in both Old and New Style. Nineteenth-century Russian dates were twelve days behind the New Style (Gregorian calendar) date, but the difference became thirteen days in the twentieth-century. Accordingly, Nabokov's birthday of April 10 1899 (Old Style), or April 22 (New Style), became, in the new century and in the revised New Style, April 23 (see *SM* 10).

1899   Vladimir Vladimirovich Nabokov born in St Petersburg, April 10/22.

1900   Birth of brother Sergei.

1901   Birth of Véra Evseevna Slonim (later Nabokov): 23 December 1901/5 January 1902.

1903   Birth of sister Olga.

1905   January: father, Vladimir Dmitrievich Nabokov, denounces 'Bloody Sunday' killings in St Petersburg City Duma.

1906   V. D. Nabokov elected to First State Duma (March); barred from politics for signing Vyborg manifesto opposing conscription and taxes (10/23 July). Birth of sister Elena.

1911   VN [Nabokov is commonly referred to by his initials] and Sergei enrol at exclusive and progressive Tenishev School. Birth of brother Kirill.

1914   VN begins to write poetry.

1915   Beginning of first love affair, with Valentina ('Liussia') Shul'gina ('Tamara' of *Speak, Memory* and 'Mary' (Mashen'ka) of *Mary*).

1916   *Stikhi (Poems)* privately printed in St Petersburg. Death of 'Uncle Ruka' (Vasiliy Rukavishnikov), who left rich estate to VN.

1917   February Revolution (27 February/12 March); V. D. Nabokov holds office in Provisional Government.

October Revolution (24–5 October/6–7 November); V. D. Nabokov sends family to Crimea (November) and escapes there himself (December).

1918   Poetry published in the volume *Dva puti (Two Paths)*, jointly authored with Andrei Balashov (Tenishev schoolmate).

V. D. Nabokov becomes Minister of Justice in Crimean Provisional Regional Government (November).

1919   Collapse of anti-Bolshevik resistance. Nabokov family sails from Sebastapol for Athens (2/15 April); arrives in London (27 May).

VN enrols at Trinity College, Cambridge, to read Natural Sciences (Zoology) and Modern and Medieval Languages (French and Russian); drops Zoology.

1920   V. D. Nabokov moves family to Berlin (August); to edit newspaper *Rul'*.

1921   VN begins to publish (poems, stories etc.) in émigré Berlin as 'Vladimir Sirin'. First-class honours in Part I of Cambridge Tripos (distinction in Russian).

1922   28 March: V. D. Nabokov assassinated, defending Cadet Party leader Pavel Miliukov from Russian monarchist extremists.

June: VN graduates from Cambridge (second-class honours); returns to Berlin and becomes engaged to Svetlana Siewert.

Translates *Alice in Wonderland* into Russian (published 1923).

December: publishes poetry collection entitled *Grozd' (The Cluster)*.

1923   January: engagement to Svetlana broken off (by her parents).

Further poetry collection published: *Gornyi put' (The Mountain Path)*.

May 8: meets Véra Evseevna Slonim at charity costume ball.

Begins writing stories on a regular basis.

VN's mother moves to Prague, with his sister Elena.

1924   Begins several years of tutoring (English, Russian, tennis, boxing).

1925   Begins first novel, *Mary* (published 1926).

15 April: marries Véra Slonim in Berlin town hall.

1926 Writes play, *The Man from the USSR*; and narrative poem, *A University Poem*.

1928 Writes *King, Queen, Knave* (published September).

1929 Writes *The Luzhin Defense* (published serially 1929–30). Publishes collection of stories and poems, *The Return of Chorb*.

1930 Completes short novel, *The Eye* (published November). Writes *Glory* (published 1931).

1931 Writes *Camera Obscura* (published 1932–3).

1932 Writes *Despair* (published 1934).

1933 Begins work on *The Gift*. Hitler comes to power; Véra loses job on closure of Jewish firm.

1934 10 May: birth of only child Dmitri. Breaks off *The Gift* to write *Invitation to a Beheading* (published 1935–6).

1935 Does his own English translation of *Despair* (published London, 1937).

1936 Writes 'Mademoiselle O' in French. Reading tour of Brussels, Antwerp, Paris. Véra loses her last German job; VN seeks job in English-speaking world.

1937 18 January: VN leaves Germany. February: Begins four-month affair with Irina Guadanini in Paris. Retranslates into English and rewrites *Camera Obscura* as *Laughter in the Dark* (published New York, 1938).

1938 January: completes *The Gift* (published serially 1937–8; but first complete edition New York, 1952). December: begins first English novel, *The Real Life of Sebastian Knight* (published USA, 1941).

1939 Death of mother in Prague (2 May). Writes novella, *The Enchanter* (published in English 1986; Russian original 1991). December: preparations begin for emigration to USA.

1940 May: Nabokovs sail to US on penultimate voyage of liner *Champlain*, arriving New York on 28 May.

1941 Offered one-year appointment in comparative literature, Wellesley College. Begins *Bend Sinister* (?).

1942 Appointed Research Fellow in Entomology, Museum of Comparative Zoology, Harvard.

1943 Completes *Nikolai Gogol* (published 1944).
1944 Appointed lecturer at Wellesley College.
Publishes *Three Russian Poets* (verse translations of Pushkin, Lermontov, Tiutchev).
1945 First story accepted by *New Yorker*.
12 July: Nabokovs become US citizens.
Hears of death of brother Sergei in Nazi concentration camp.
1946 Completes *Bend Sinister* (published 1947).
1947 Plans *Lolita* and autobiography. *Nine Stories* published.
1948 Appointed as professor of Russian Literature, Cornell University.
1949 Introduces Russian Poetry, English and Russian survey courses, and Pushkin seminar.
1950 Completes *Conclusive Evidence* (published 1951; revised in Russian 1954).
Begins writing *Lolita*.
Introduces courses in European fiction and Russian literature in translation.
1951 Writes 'The Vane Sisters' (published 1959); and last short story, 'Lance' (published 1952).
1952 Visiting Lecturer at Harvard.
1953 Serious work launched on *Eugene Onegin* commentaries.
Begins writing *Pnin*. Completes *Lolita*.
1955 Sends *Lolita* manuscript to European agent; published Paris, 1955. Completes *Pnin* (published 1957).
1956 Puts finishing touches to Dmitri's translation of Lermontov's *A Hero of Our Time* (published 1958).
1957 Begins *Pale Fire*. Completes edition of *Eugene Onegin* (published 1964).
1958 *Lolita* published in US, selling 100,000 in first three weeks.
Publishes *Nabokov's Dozen* (short stories).
1959 19 January: delivers last Cornell lecture.
Completes translation of *Song of Igor's Campaign* (published 1960).
Publishes *Poems* and co-translation (with Dmitri) of *Invitation to a Beheading* (first co-'Englishing', with Dmitri and others, of the earlier Russian novels).
British edition of *Lolita* (published 6 November).
1960 Writes *Lolita* screenplay for Stanley Kubrick in California.

1961   October: moves to Hotel Montreux Palace (Montreux, Switzerland).

        December: completes *Pale Fire* (published 1962).

1962   June: attends premiere of Kubrick's *Lolita* in New York.

1963   Revises *Eugene Onegin* translation for publication of 4-volume edition (1964).

1964   Resumes work on 'The Texture of Time' and Russian translation of *Lolita*.

1965   Completes Russian *Lolita* (published New York, 1967; first publication in Russia, 1991). Revises his own 1936 translation of *Despair*.

        Cancels long-standing project on 'Butterflies of Europe'.

1966   Completes revision of *Speak, Memory* (published 1967).

        Links 'The Texture of Time' with serious work on *Ada*.

1968   Completes *Ada* (published 1969).

1969   Begins writing *Transparent Things*.

1970   Publishes *Poems and Problems*.

1971   Begins translation of Russian stories (with Dmitri) for further collections.

1972   Completes *Transparent Things* (published October).

1973   January–February: corrects manuscript of Andrew Field's *Nabokov. His Life in Part*.

        March: Begins writing *Look at the Harlequins!*

        Publishes *A Russian Beauty and Other Stories* and *Strong Opinions*.

1974   April: finishes *Look at the Harlequins!* (published August).

        Publishes *Lolita. A Screenplay*.

        Maps out a new novel, *The Original of Laura* (never completed).

1975   Publishes *Tyrants Destroyed and Other Stories*.

        Revised edition of *Eugene Onegin* published.

1976   Publishes *Details of a Sunset and Other Stories*.

1977   2 July: dies in hospital in Lausanne.

Preface

To fiction be as to your country true.

(G 145)

Vladimir Nabokov's reputation, in terms of his achievement in establishing himself as a major writer in two literatures, is all but unique in western culture. Joseph Conrad – a novelist of whom Nabokov thought little – springs to some minds as a comparable figure, but he wrote only in an English that was, to all intents and purposes, his third language. A closer analogue – and a figure of whom Nabokov thought rather more – is Samuel Beckett. In any case, being dismissed by Nabokov – who was notorious for his 'strong' and idiosyncratic opinions (see the collection he called *Strong Opinions*) on literature, as on much else – was no guarantee against having had a certain impact on him.

Nabokov (1899–1977) is the author of seventeen novels and sixty-five stories, many of which exist in double versions – Russian–English, or English–Russian: if not originally authored in both languages, then authorized by him through collaborative translation (mostly with his son Dmitri). He began writing as a poet in Tsarist Russia, but progressed to prose fiction in emigration, under the name of Sirin, switching languages (to both English and French) even before his wartime flight to the United States. He subsequently liked to consider himself, however, as first and foremost an American novelist, even – or especially – after moving residence back to Europe. He was the author too of autobiography, plays, a not insubstantial body of criticism, a number of translations, chess problems, and learned studies in lepidoptery.

Nabokov, who always claimed 'I think in images' (*SO* 14), prided himself on his mastery of prose style in two of the

xi

world's foremost literary languages and his *oeuvre* remains, as one consequence, the happiest of hunting grounds for narrative theorists, exponents of intertextuality, and sleuths of the hidden patterning, the signs and symbols behind the surface plots. These vary in emphasis from the trauma through transference of exile, to the intellectualized thriller, to the dissection of obsession, to the exploration of alternative worlds. The recreation of lost love and the magic of childhood is a prominent concern; problems of memory and knowledge are a constant; style and story are the dominant: 'the good writer is first of all an enchanter', he wrote to Edmund Wilson (*N–W* 177). Stylistic, structural, and indeed cultural dexterity are his hallmarks; his cultural debts, in an order that is no simple task to determine, are to Russia, to Europe, to America, and to the British Isles; geographically (and chronologically) it is an easier matter: the principal staging posts are St Petersburg, Cambridge, Berlin, Paris, Cornell (Ithaca, New York), and Montreux.

Now that we have arrived at the landmark of the Nabokov centenary, it is high time to take stock, not only of Nabokov's works themselves, but of the large body of criticism, now approaching almost Joycean proportions, accumulated by the enchanted hunters of Nabokov scholarship; a brief summary of their labours is to be found at the end of Chapter 1, and many of them are referred to in passing, or in endnotes, elsewhere.

Film versions of his most controversial novel keep Nabokov's name before the public, as does the threat of legal action against publication of an English translation of a certain novel called *Lo's Diary* (by an Italian writer named Pia Pera). *Lolita*, indeed, ranked fourth in the 1998 New York Modern Library list of the hundred best novels of the century published in English. At the same time, almost the entire Nabokovian *oeuvre* remains currently available (in the UK and elsewhere) in paperback and, in addition, has finally found its native readership in Russia.

Nabokov's lofty reputation does not, then, rest only on *Lolita* – according to Edmund White, 'the supreme novel of love in the twentieth century'.[1] Far from it; and we attempt here to follow (in White's words) 'our freshest landscape painter in words' ever deeper into 'the luminous unknown'[2] of wordplay and worldplay, into realms in which patterned complexity and the ludic blend with the ethical and the metaphysical, and in which

xii

'aesthetic bliss' (*pace* Nabokov himself: *L* 314) may not be the only pursuit. His range is far wider than the (supposedly) erotic: as for *Lolita*, Frank Kermode noted a decade ago that 'nowadays it is commonly praised for its reticence',[3] and it is in any case exceeded in its eroticism (in most estimations, at least) by the late novel, *Ada*. The author of a number of short-story masterpieces, Nabokov wrote the one great Russian émigré novel (*The Gift*), and achieved the remarkable feat of basing one of the most acclaimed American novels of the century on an eccentric commentary to an original English narrative poem. In his last phase, he progressed through the extended virtuosic demonism of *Ada* to the more disciplined dementia of *Look at the Harlequins!* (an effective, if unintended, swansong). These are just a few of the peaks achieved by a man who was dubbed by David Lodge 'very much a "writer's writer"', and a vital influence on a number of our most distinguished contemporary novelists – Martin Amis and John Banville being just two prominent examples.[4]

Nevertheless, let us return, though of course only briefly at this juncture, to *Lolita*. How can Edmund White call this work, ostensibly the confession of a monstrous debaucher, 'the supreme novel of love in the twentieth century'? There is a reading of the novel by which Humbert Humbert, the old European (poetic and academic) predator on the young Miss America is spiritually, at least in some sense, 'saved' from his obsession with nymphetry by his love for the 'mature' (17-year-old and pregnant) Lolita (or rather, perhaps, is 'saved' *by* Lolita). It is, though, a reading at face value. But *Lolita* is, as White himself stresses, 'full of parodies', not least 'of earlier love novels';[5] as ever, to Nabokov, 'the writer's pulpit is dangerously close to the pulp romance' (*LL* 376). Nothing, arguably at least, is as it seems; 'Cue' Quilty, for instance, as Robert Adams has pointed out, may be merely 'a phantom of Humbert Humbert's insanely guilty, insanely jealous, imagination'.[6] These and other problems of narration, identity, chronology, reflection, and cognition will be discussed in their due place (on this text, in Chapter 5: 'The *Lolita* Phenomenon'). In any event, throughout his career (to lean again momentarily on White), 'it was Nabokov's particular delight to invent sinister or insane or talentless versions of himself, characters who are at least in part mocking anticipations of naive readers' suspicions about the real Nabokov'.[7] Just one emblem of this is to be found in the (fictitious) John Ray, Jr.'s 'Foreword' to *Lolita*: the (anagrammatic) Vivian Darkbloom's 'biography' of Quilty, *My Cue* (*L* 4), surely corresponds at some alternative level to a supposable '*Mon cul!* by Vladimir Nabokov'.

Acknowledgements

The author and publishers are pleased to acknowledge the inclusion of quotations from Nabokov's works and additional writings, the sources of which are detailed in the bibliography.

For her advice and encouragement in matters Nabokovian, I am grateful to Priscilla Meyer. For answering queries and/or assistance with materials, I have to thank Ignat Avsey, Gennadi Barabtarlo, Birgit Beumers, George Donaldson, Ronald Knowles, Priscilla Meyer, Stephen Jan Parker, and Michael Pursglove; and, for mercurial reading and incisive comment, Maggie Malone.

Abbreviations and References

All quotations from Nabokov's works are taken from the Penguin editions, except those listed otherwise below (for fuller details, see Bibliography).

A	*Ada or Ardor: A Family Chronicle.*
BS	*Bend Sinister.*
CSVN	*Collected Stories* [styled on title page *The Stories of Vladimir Nabokov*].
E	*The Enchanter*, transl. by Dmitri Nabokov (London: Picador, 1986).
G	*The Gift.*
DS	*Details of a Sunset and Other Stories.*
L	*The Annotated Lolita.*
LATH	*Look at the Harlequins!*
LDQ	*Lectures on Don Quixote*, ed. by Fredson Bowers (London: Weidenfeld and Nicolson, 1983).
LL	*Lectures on Literature*, ed. by Fredson Bowers (London: Weidenfeld and Nicolson, 1980).
LRL	*Lectures on Russian Literature*, ed. by Fredson Bowers (London: Weidenfeld and Nicolson, 1982).
LS	*Lolita: A Screenplay*, in *Novels 1955–1962: Lolita, Pnin, Pale Fire, Lolita: A Screenplay* (New York: The Library of America, 1996).
M	*Mary.*
ND	*Nabokov's Dozen.*
NG	*Nikolai Gogol* (New York: New Directions, 1961).
N–W	*The Nabokov–Wilson Letters, 1940–71*, ed. by Simon Karlinsky (New York: Harper and Row, 1979).
P	*Pnin.*

PF   *Pale Fire.*
PP   *Poems and Problems* (New York: McGraw-Hill, 1970).
RB   *A Russian Beauty and Other Stories.*
RLSK   *The Real Life of Sebastian Knight.*
SL   *Selected Letters, 1940–77*, ed. by Dmitri Nabokov and
          Matthew J. Bruccoli (London: Vintage, 1991).
SM   *Speak, Memory.*
Stikhi   *Stikhi* [Verses] (Ann Arbor: Ardis, 1979).
SO   *Strong Opinions* (London: Weidenfeld and Nicolson,
          1974).
TD   *Tyrants Destroyed and Other Stories.*

References in the text to abbreviated critical studies and
collections are to the following editions:

B Am   Brian Boyd, *Vladimir Nabokov: The American Years*
          (London: Chatto and Windus, 1992).
B Rus   Brian Boyd, *Vladimir Nabokov: The Russian Years*
          (London: Chatto and Windus, 1990).
5th Arc   *Nabokov's Fifth Arc: Nabokov and Others on his Life's Work,*
          ed. by J. E. Rivers and Charles Nicol (Austin: University
          of Texas Press, 1982).
GCVN   *The Garland Companion to Vladimir Nabokov,* ed. by
          Vladimir E. Alexandrov (New York: Garland, 1995).
NS   *Nabokov Studies* [journal, 1994–].
Q   *Vladimir Nabokov: A Tribute,* ed. by Peter Quennell
          (London: Weidenfeld and Nicolson, 1979).
RLT   *Russian Literature Triquarterly* [journal, 1972–1991].
Things   *A Book of Things About Vladimir Nabokov,* ed. by Carl R.
          Proffer (Ann Arbor: Ardis, 1974).

1

Introduction: A VN Survey

I would suggest 'talk of' or 'balk of' as more closely related to the stressed middle vowel of that awkward name ('Nabawkof'). I once composed the following rhyme for my students:

> The querulous gawk of
> A heron at night
> Prompts Nabokov
> To write

(SO 302)

'Mr Nabórkov', 'Mr Nabáhkov', 'Mr Nabkov', or 'Mr Nabóhkov' are versions of attempts at pronouncing his name mentioned by Vladimir Nabokov in a 1964 interview (SO 24). The authentic Russian-sounding 'Nabawkof' was reiterated in 1970. By the time of 'The Last Interview' with Robert Robinson for the BBC, however, Nabokov complains that 'American autograph seekers...rejuggle the vowels of my name in all the ways allowed by mathematics. "Nabakav" is especially touching for the "a"s.' 'Nabarkov' is said to be favoured by New Yorkers, 'while the aberration, "Nabokov" is a favourite one of postal officials'. Now, though, Nabokov claims (in February 1977), 'I've settled for the euphonious "Nabokov", with the middle syllable accented and rhyming with "smoke"' (Q 121). Up until his emigration to America, VN (as Nabokov has commonly been called) spelled his surname 'Nabokoff'. Now that Nabokov, in his works, has at last returned to his native Russia, we should think of his name in its original pronunciation:

> So now let us talk of
> Vladeemir Nabawkof

Vladimir Vladimirovich Nabokov was born in St Petersburg in 1899, into a wealthy aristocratic family with a lengthy and

1

distinguished history of court, political, and military connections. Allegedly descended from a Russianized Tartar prince (Nabok Murza), the Nabokov dynasty remained untitled, twice when offered the choice 'between the title of count [*graf*] and a sum of money, presumably large', choosing the latter (*SM* 47). In the best traditions of the liberal Russian intelligentsia, the Nabokovs of the turn of the twentieth century were steeped in Russian and European culture, and their fortunate children were instructed by resident tutors and governesses of various nationalities. A veritable army of servants – maids, footmen, lackeys, coachmen, chauffeurs, and gardeners, whose children could be called on as ballboys for tennis (*SM* 34) – spanning the extensive city and country properties, were presided over, as we gather from Nabokov's autobiography *Speak, Memory*, by those most benevolent of despots, the Nabokov parents. Well over half a century later, having returned to a life of luxury following several decades of relative penury, Nabokov gave as the reason for protracted residence in a Swiss hotel his inability 'to visualize an adequate staff', given that '[o]ld retainers require time to get old' (*Q* 122-3). The retinue of servants depicted on the Ardis estate in *Ada* were scarcely any wild exaggeration. Nabokov was not, though, totally oblivious to the impression he might have created; he refers to his youthful pose *en route* for the Crimea as that of 'a brittle young fop' (*SM* 188), while his portrait of the arrogant Van Veen in *Ada* plays on similar sensibilities.

Nabokov always stressed his 'English' upbringing, which he dated virtually from the cradle: 'I was bilingual as a baby' (*SO* 5); 'I was an English child' (*SO* 81); 'I was a perfectly normal trilingual child in a family with a large library' (*SO* 43). French was soon added to English and Russian, while literacy in the language of his native land was soon found to be lagging behind a precocious proficiency in written English. What Nabokov frequently referred to as his 'magical' childhood did indeed have something of the fairy tale about it: his rich maternal 'Uncle Ruka' left him an even larger fortune in 1916 – though his enjoyment of this was, of course, to be shortlived. Foreign travel – by 'pile-carpeted international express trains' (*SM* 126) to Abbazia, Biarritz, Berlin, or Wiesbaden – and summers on the country estate had been the norm. Private tutors were augmented by an exclusive St Petersburg private school. Wide reading, entomology, and chess soon had to compete with forwardness with the opposite sex and the writing of poetry. The 18-year-old Nabokov was already a published poet and an experienced lover by the time the October Revolution and civil war brought his idyllic and privileged world crashing down.

The prominent role of Vladimir Dmitrievich Nabokov in constitutional-democratic politics meant both that the family had no choice but to emigrate, and that they were fortunate in accomplishing this intact (even the 'final dachsund followed us into exile': *SM* 40). They were never to return to Russia. The Crimean interlude and the early years in emigration were financed by the sale of family jewels, thanks to the foresight of trusty servants (money and mail had been heroically delivered to Yalta by a former chauffeur), subsequently helped out by émigré benevolent funds. The two elder boys were thus enabled to study at Cambridge. Having settled at first in London, the Nabokov family moved in 1920 to Berlin, then a major centre of émigré cultural and political life.

Disaster, however, struck in 1922, when V. D. Nabokov flung himself in front of an even more prominent political leader in exile, Pavel Miliukov, and was thereby assassinated by Russian right-wing monarchist fanatics. Vladimir Nabokov was reading Blok's *Italian Verses* to his mother at the precise instant that the phone rang reporting his father's murder. Shortly after this, he graduated from Cambridge and settled into literary life in Russian Berlin, where he began serious writing and supplemented his living by tutoring or coaching in languages and sports. After one broken engagement he met Véra Slonim, whom he married in 1925. Literary recognition began to come later that decade, as the works of 'V. Sirin', Nabokov's pen-name (adopted partly to avoid confusion with his father), attracted wide attention in émigré literary circles, by now centred principally on Paris, and began to be translated into German.[1]

Nabokov's mother (Elena Ivanovna, *née* Rukavishnikov) had moved with daughter Elena to Prague (where she was to die in 1939). Nabokov, despite fifteen years of residence in Germany, claimed never to have learned German (although his professed ignorance of that language may well have been somewhat exaggerated).[2] The rise to power of the Nazis made Germany an ever less congenial environment for the Nabokovs, who by now had a son (Dmitri, born in 1934); this was particularly so as Véra Nabokov was herself of Russian Jewish origin and the firms for whom she worked tended to be closed down. Nabokov travelled to give readings in Paris and Brussels and began to write in, or to translate himself into, both French and English. He also started the process of seeking academic employment in both England and the United States. In 1937 a Paris affair threatened his marriage, but the arrival of his family in France resulted in renewed and permanent marital stability. Eventually the offer of a summer-school post at Stanford allowed the Nabokovs to obtain visas to leave for America in 1940. The ship on which they sailed, the *Champlain*, was sunk on its very next voyage.

Nabokov arrived in the United States with a large body of prepared lectures on Russian and European literature. He held temporary academic posts for a number of years, researched into lepidoptery at Harvard (undertaking field trips across the States in vacations), and began to publish works in English. A stimulating literary friendship with Edmund Wilson lasted, on and off, through most of the Nabokovs' two American decades. A tenured professorship at Cornell provided welcome security as Nabokov's parallel careers (as writer, academic, and entomologist) began to flourish. Outwardly renouncing Russian as a working language, he continued to write poetry in Russian, as well as publishing a version of his autobiography (*Conclusive Evidence*, 1951, later to be 'revisited' as *Speak, Memory*, 1967), as *Drugie berega* ('Other Shores'), in 1954. His controversial novel *Lolita* proved difficult to publish and Nabokov resorted to the Olympia Press in Paris (which published it in 1955) before Putnam's took the plunge in the United States, to critical acclaim and financial triumph, in 1958.

The rapid return to affluence, brought about by *Lolita*'s bestselling status, enabled Nabokov to resign from Cornell, in order to concentrate fully on his three main literary pursuits: the composition of further novels, the completion of his translation projects from Russian literature, and the translation (or the supervision thereof) of his own Russian works into English (and subsequently of *Lolita* into Russian). After exploratory visits to Europe, the Nabokovs settled into what was to become their permanent base: an apartment in the Palace Hotel in Montreux, Switzerland. Having taken American citizenship in 1945, however, Nabokov continued to express a feeling of belonging to what he still considered his adopted country: 'I am an American writer, born in Russia and educated in England where I studied French literature, before spending fifteen years in Germany', he declared in his *Playboy* interview of 1964 (*SO* 26). A subsequent letter signed by 'Mrs Vladimir Nabokov' advised an American librarian of her husband's preference for his books to be shelved under American literature, 'since his best work was done in English' (*SL* 454). To the last (in the BBC interview only months before his death), Nabokov declared 'I will certainly return to the United States at the first opportunity' (*Q* 123). This was not to be.

At his death in July 1977, Nabokov left a number of 'un-Englished' (and some unpublished) early short stories; these have recently been translated and published by Dmitri Nabokov, and are included in the *Collected Stories* (*CSVN*). A second volume of autobiography, to have been entitled 'Speak on, Memory' remained unwritten. He did, though, leave one last novel, *The Original of Laura*, described by him towards the end of 1976 as a 'not quite finished manuscript' (*SL* 562) and by Dmitri as what 'would have been Father's most brilliant novel, the most concentrated distillation of his creativity, but whose release in incomplete form he expressly forbade' (*Q* 129).[3]

Sport and chess were among Nabokov's favoured pursuits, along with lepidoptery, and these all featured in a number of his works. He included a memorable description of keeping goal for Trinity College in *Speak, Memory*, an activity duplicated by Martin Edelweiss, the protagonist of *Glory*; and he gave the English title 'Football' to a Russian poem written at Cambridge (*Stikhi*, 24–5). He continued to keep goal into the 1930s in Germany and, in much later life, would break his policy of no television in the home for important soccer competitions. A keen exponent of fisticuffs from his schooldays, Nabokov boxed at Cambridge (reflected in the fight between Martin and his friend Darwin in *Glory*), and later gave boxing lessons in Berlin, engaging in exhibition bouts to drum up pupils. He even gave a talk to a Russian literary circle, his biographer Brian Boyd tells us, 'on the beauty of sport and on the art of boxing in particular' – including 'the pleasant sensation of being knocked out on the chin' (*B Rus* 257). He played tennis for most of his life and this too has its fictional moments (as in the early story 'La Veneziana' and in *Lolita*). There is even evidence that he took some interest in cricket. Nabokov devised and published chess problems, and this game all but dominates his third novel, *The Luzhin Defense*. He also credits himself with creating the first Russian crossword puzzles (and coining the word *krestoslovitsa*, as opposed to the Soviet usage, *krossvord*: *SM* 217; *B Am* 241).

A potentially more lethal activity (than being knocked out either boxing or goalkeeping – both of which happened to Nabokov) was duelling. Ingrained in the traditions of aristocratic and literary Russia, the duel had figured too in Nabokov family history. *Speak, Memory* (147–51) includes an impressionable account by the twelve-year-old Vladimir of the circumstances surrounding a duel – not, in the event, fought by his father. Relics of this custom persisted in some European countries, at least into the early years of Russian émigré life, and Nabokov several times challenged, or considered challenging (or was himself almost called out by), 'opponents' on matters of personal or literary honour to duels which (fortunately) never took place. Duels, or the theme of duelling, are occasionally represented too in his fiction, most notably perhaps in the story 'An Affair of Honor' (written 1927), and copious notes on the subject were to be included in the commentaries to *Eugene Onegin*. Even in his American years he would still wryly exploit this cultural memory: '"Ah, a duel!" Nabokov had exclaimed, when [Professor Robert Martin] Adams appeared at the [Cornell] departmental office one morning with his newly broken arm in a sling' (*Q* 15).

Nabokov's lifelong passion for lepidoptery is eloquently described in Chapter Six of *Speak, Memory* and a rich assortment of butterflies and moths flutter through his *œuvre*. From early childhood, as he puts it, 'I discovered in nature the nonutilitarian delights that I sought in art' (*SM* 98). In particular, these were nature's propensities for mimicry, camouflage and metamorphosis. Moreover, he makes occasional or cameo appearances in a number of works, somewhat in the manner of Alfred Hitchcock, and often in the emblematic guise of a rambling lepidopterist. Such a 'representative' (as he dubbed authorial 'guests', in the 1935 story 'Recruiting') may bear an anagrammatic version of Nabokov's own name (such as 'Blavdak Vinomori' in his second

6

novel, *King, Queen, Knave*), or the disguise may be a little less or a little more distinctive.

In addition to 'Sirin', early Nabokov publications appeared under such affectations as 'Cantab.' or 'V. Cantaboff', while he signed a letter to his mother 'Dorian Vivalcomb' and invented an English dramatist named 'Vivian Calmbrood' (whose works he pretended to translate (see, for instance, *Stikhi* 238-42)). Later suchlike manifestations were to include the androgynous 'Vivian Darkbloom': mistress and biographer of Clare Quilty in *Lolita*, who subsequently doubles as annotator of *Ada* ('a shy violet in Cambridge', playfully included by Nabokov in a 1971 list of critics considered to have 'added their erudition to my inspiration, with brilliant results': *SO* 192). These inventions of pseudonyms, varieties of *alter ego*, or self-representations, signal a concern with identity and doubling on various levels, and herald the pursuit of fictitious biography, or autobiography, that was to emerge as a prominent feature of Nabokov's work, from *The Real Life of Sebastian Knight*, through *Pale Fire*, to *Look at the Harlequins!* Indeed, virtually all Nabokov's main works permutate this theme. It is fitting that he should himself have been on the receiving end of false identities: as an infant he was almost christened 'Victor' by mistake, while a group photograph of Parisian *literati* taken in 1937 wrongly identifies Nabokov as the French writer Jacques Audiberti (*SM* 19, 7).

The naturalist in combination with the landscape painter – this was how Nabokov saw his artistic approach; and the visual arts, minutely observed detail, modes of perception, and angles of vision all contribute to mosaic or kaleidoscopic effect. As a small boy, 'climbing into the picture above my bed', inspired by an English fairy tale once read by his mother, was an imagined fancy of Nabokov's (*SM* 68). In later works, both picture and fairy-tale (or 'enchantment') motifs would be repeated and elaborated (notably, for instance, in *Glory*). The cinema and paintings (indeed in combination, in the form of a proposed cinematic animation of old masters) would form one motif of *Laughter in the Dark*. Life as chess would provide a framework for *The Luzhin Defense*, again with pictorial references, while a section of *Speak, Memory* draws a clear analogy between patterning in chess, fiction and life (*SM* 221–5). Theatrical trappings play their part in the structure of *Invitation to a*

7

Beheading, and allusions to circus and other performance arts and artists (actors, acrobats, film extras and harlequins) are scattered through many works. Nabokov himself took casual walk-on film work in Berlin and wrote cabaret sketches and pantomimes. The practice of walking on one's hands (later attributed to Ganin in *Mary* and performed by Van Veen in *Ada*) owes its probable inspiration to 'a large, formidably athletic Lett', one of many tutors supervising the Nabokov boys (*SM* 123). Indeed, the seeds of much of Nabokov's imagery and many of his devices are to be located in his childhood – at least as we know it from *Speak, Memory*.

A poem written as early as 1919, in Crimea, contains the lines:

> The far-off crests of future works, amidst
> the shadows of my soul are still concealed
> like mountaintops in pre-auroral mist.

> (*PP* 22–3)

There is a sense in which Nabokov, like his literary 'representative' Fyodor Godunov-Cherdyntsev in *The Gift*, anticipated or even 'remembered' his future works. The motif of the harlequin, in its varied application, which is brought to the fore, as we shall see, in his last completed novel, arose from childhood distractions during Mademoiselle's readings, duly recorded in *Speak, Memory*:

> On the white window ledges, on the long window seats covered with faded calico, the sun breaks into geometrical gems after passing through rhomboids and squares of stained glass.... But the most constant source of enchantment during those readings came from the harlequin pattern of colored panes inset in a whitewashed framework on either side of the veranda. (*SM* 83–4)

The harlequin's wooden sword has already become the instrument of the poet, as 'he taps his knee with his wandlike pencil' for inspiration at the very start of the 15-year-old Nabokov's poetic career (*SM* 169). Almost at the distant end of his career, noting the critical disapproval with which *Look at the Harlequins!* had largely been greeted, he penned the following lines (in Russian and, as always, 'to Véra'):

> Oh, they send them packing to the Steppes, my Harlequins,
> into the coombs, to alien chieftains!
> Their geometry, their Venetian qualities
> they call buffoonery and deception.

Only you, only you kept your amazement
at the black, blue and orange rhomboids...
'N is an outstanding writer, a snob and an athlete,
endowed with immense aplomb...'

(*Stikhi* 299; translation mine)

Also during the Crimean hiatus, Nabokov reports, together with a companion:

parodizing a biographic approach projected, as it were, into the future and thus transforming the very specious present into a kind of paralyzed past as perceived by a doddering memoirist who recalls, through a helpless haze, his acquaintance with a great writer when both were young. (*SM* 191–2)

The recalled sample of ensuing repartee may not be over-stimulating, but here again the seeds (or the 'perverse and spiteful demon': *SM* 192) of future Nabokovian structure are evident. Time in Nabokov is the essence: 'I confess I do not believe in time. I like to fold my magic carpet, after use, in such a way as to superimpose one part of the pattern upon another. Let visitors trip' (*SM* 109). 'The future is but the obsolete in reverse', we are told in the late short story 'Lance' (*ND* 165). In Crimea too, Boyd tells us, Nabokov wrote a one-act playlet (entitled 'Vesnoi': 'In Spring'), whose characters include a chess player and a youth, the latter 'in fact the chess player as a young man' (*B Rus* 141). Localized harlequinesque patterns of colour and object will be juxtaposed with larger scale patterns in time and space, to produce 'cosmic synchronization' – a term attributed to 'Vivian Bloodmark, a philosophical friend of mine' (*SM* 169) – or what amounts to a kind of temporal abseiling: '...that day nobody (*except my older self*) could see me shake out a piece of twig in an otherwise empty net and stare at a hole in the tarlatan' (*SM* 105; emphasis mine). Memory is the vital conduit, and the whole may be expressed to synaesthetic effect (an approach originally encouraged in the young Nabokov by his mother): memory's 'supreme achievement...is the masterly use it makes of innate harmonies when gathering to its fold the suspended and wandering tonalities of the past' (*SM* 134).

Following on from memory, loss is, not surprisingly, another pre-eminent theme in Nabokov. Typically, he was writing juvenilia on loss even before anything had been lost: 'my elegy dealt with the loss of a beloved mistress...whom I had never lost, never loved, never met but was all set to meet, love lose' (*SM* 175). Soon, however, there were mistresses to lose, plus the loss of Russia and, in a sense, of the Russian language. It was the loss of Russia, followed by the sudden and violent loss of his father, and later that of his brother (Sergei Nabokov died in a German concentration camp in 1945, arrested first as a homosexual and then as an English spy) that are variously reflected and refracted through Nabokov's works. And it was the switching of literary languages that transformed his artistic career.

History, politics, and social themes are avowedly eschewed by Nabokov, although he could write on such matters with a terse and telling effect if he so chose. For that matter, totalitarianism is a target of direct artistic attack in the novels *Invitation to a Beheading* and *Bend Sinister*, plus the story 'Tyrants Destroyed', and such issues inevitably retain an at least inferential presence elsewhere. The Russian Revolution and the Holocaust left deep scars on Nabokov and he was equally scathing in his attitude to the Bolsheviks and the Nazis – and their respective fellow-travellers. He continued to think of himself as 'an old-fashioned liberal' (*SO* 96), a (self-styled, apolitical) democratic republican who could condone McCarthyism in the United States (given that it was directed against communists) but was implacably opposed to capital punishment (to which end he had, in part at least, devoted his novel *Invitation to a Beheading*). He remained all his life a fiercely independent 'non-joiner' (or so he liked to claim).[4] Notwithstanding his cold-war sympathies, Nabokov authorized Véra to write on his behalf in 1972 that 'Nazi control of the world would have been worse, [than the international situation then pertaining] and not only because of Hitler's mad-dog policy toward the Jews' (*SL* 497). Nevertheless, Nabokov prefers to outdo the Stephen Dedalus view of history in *Ulysses*, as 'a nightmare from which I am trying to awake', with his own – ultra-Nabokovian – comment, that his family's enforced migrations were occasioned as 'the shadow of fool-made history vitiated even the exactitude of sundials' (*SM* 234). Meanwhile, he developed, in unique fashion, the art of turning successive stages of 'the gloom and the glory of exile' (*SM* 214) to his own artistic advantage.

In his Cambridge years, Nabokov had a morbid fear of 'losing or corrupting' his command of Russian – 'the only thing I had salvaged from Russia'; this he found more harassing than the later fear 'of my never being able to bring my English prose anywhere close to the level of my Russian' (*SM* 204). In 1954, after recomposing *Conclusive Evidence* in Russian, he recalled 'what agony it was, in the early 'forties, to switch from Russian to English' (although, in the late thirties, as we have noted, he had been writing more or less simultaneously in his three languages), and that he had then sworn never to 'go back from my wizened Hyde form to my ample Jekyll one' (*SL* 149). This had not, of course, stopped him from continuing, albeit almost furtively, to 'relapse' into the occasional composition of Russian verse. In her study of bilingual Russian writers, Elizabeth Beaujour sees bilingualism (or, in his case, trilingualism) as crucial from the beginning for Nabokov, and she notes that the language in which he composed his literary works was, for extended periods of his life, '*not* the ambient language of the place where he was physically located', that he reverted to putting his real name to his works 'only after he had accepted his destiny as a polyglot writer', and that even then 'he continued to use narrators for whom English (particularly American English) is not the first language'.[5] It may also be noted that in Cambridge, for instance, Nabokov would play the Russian card, while in Germany his pose would tend to be that of the Englishman.

When he did switch to writing in English, Nabokov fully (some would say excessively) exploited his extensive linguistic and cultural polyglot facility. This, it is universally agreed, contributed to and strongly coloured the striking originality of his English prose style, impinging as well on character, setting, and content. *The Real Life of Sebastian Knight* touches on the problematics of a Russian writing in English; *Bend Sinister* introduces an invented (hybrid) language and other elements of paronomasia (code-switching or wordplay). Richness of vocabulary, unusual turns of expression, defamiliarization, and what Boyd calls 'phonic patter and cryptic pattern' (*B Rus* 152) are to the fore. These qualities are displayed to a further degree in *Lolita* and the later novels, together with complex narrative schemes and an increasingly self-referential tendency. In *Ada*, as

Beaujour puts it, 'Nabokov allows himself to behave linguistically very much as polyglots behave when they communicate with each other, rather than with monoglot speakers of any of their languages'.[6] This brings Nabokov to his closest proximity (though still a relatively restrained proximity) to the Joyce of *Finnegans Wake* – which, as it happens, he appreciated least of the Joycean *oeuvre*. Some reviewers and commentators decided that Nabokov here reaches unseemly heights of self-indulgence. Others, however, persevere, either choosing to see such linguistic and inter-referential experimentation in a positive light, or believing that Nabokov criticism is too important to leave to the polyglots.

In her preface to the collection of Nabokov's verse published in 1979, Véra Nabokov emphasized what she considered Nabokov's 'main theme' which, although 'everything he wrote was saturated with it', she claimed, had been noticed by no one; this was the theme of *potustoronnost'* (literally to do with being 'on the other side') – variously translated as the 'otherworld', the 'beyond', or the 'hereafter' (*Stikhi* 3). While this concept within Nabokov's work had not gone completely unremarked, it had certainly not received the attention she felt to be its due. This shortfall has by now been made perhaps more than good, as something of an 'otherworld' bandwagon has been rolling for some time in Nabokov scholarship. The concept of the otherworld (or a dualistic system in which some sort of survival into a dimension beyond death is posited) is, or can also be, linked with what has been called 'the "Ultima Thule" theme' in Nabokov (deriving from the story of that name): the possible possession of some ultimately cosmos-shaking and incommunicable secret of the universe.[7]

While Nabokov expressed a constant hostility to any organized religion (consistently referring to Russian Orthodoxy, for instance, as 'the Greek Catholic Church': *SM* 32 and elsewhere), he was clearly captivated by possibilities, or intimations, of immortality, and this question is variously treated throughout his works. Nabokov's aesthetics, ethics, and metaphysics may be seen to form a continuum – an interlinking of art, nature, and the otherworld hinted at through epiphanic moments, patterned details of repetition, or fatidic dates or numerals. Inspiration and imagination are linked to transcendence and timelessness.

Mimicry and deception are ever-vital ingredients. Nabokov's 'highest benchmark', according to Vladimir Alexandrov, is 'consciousness on the level of cosmic synchronization.'[8] Survival, or a possibility thereof, into posthumous realms or another dimension is conjured with, as even are ghostly influences on, or supervision over, the human world. An author's-eye view of meticulously amassed material may be equated with a God's-eye view of life and the universe. Much of the time the metaphysical concerns in Nabokov's works are deeply buried, or ironically and ambiguously presented; the ultimate truth is in any case deemed to be unknowable. Whilst seeking 'to dismantle the widespread critical view' that Nabokov 'is first and foremost a metaliterary writer' and to promote instead 'an aesthetic rooted in...intuition of a transcendent realm' as 'the basis of his art', Alexandrov himself at times appears to sustain the at least equal validity of the metafictional stance, speaking of 'a dualistic world view in which the transcendent authors the mundane world', or the implication that 'human life is like a book authored by a transcendent realm'.[9]

An otherworld predilection in Nabokov's fictional and non-fictional writings is not, of course, to be denied. The question is rather: what is to be made of it, either as a whole, or in particular instances? The 'otherworldists' in Nabokov scholarship may discern a broadly religious shade, though usually of a Gnostic, a Neoplatonist or a *sui generis* hue, rather than a (clearly untenable) Christian or Orthodox one. The concern with transcending time is reminiscent of eastern philosophy, although Nabokov is not known to have been versed in this; the impulse at times may be towards immortality through art, or the exploration of models of immortality, or of alternative (or 'possible') worlds. 'Byzantine imagery' was developed by Nabokov in verse of the 1920s, he claimed, solely for 'literary stylization' (*SO* 160). So we return, in a circle or a spiral, to literary and metafictional practice and motivation, as Nabokov's concerns with the epistemological and the ontological (or with memory and hints of another world) sit conveniently with recent theories of modernism, late modernism, and postmodernism.[10]

Do Nabokov's aesthetics derive from his metaphysics, or are his metaphysics rather to be seen as a part of his aesthetics? The

13

critical emphasis on these particularities may legitimately vary. Investigation of otherworld issues in Nabokov will certainly contribute to bringing out what Alexandrov regards as 'the hidden depths in his works'; however, it is doubtful whether the wholesale detection of spiritual revenants or interventions in virtually every breeze or form of natural life really enhances the literary value of Nabokov's fictional masterworks.[11] The present study will tend to stress unashamedly the metafictional, while endeavouring to retain within view at least a semblance of the metaphysical.

This is a convenient point at which to introduce an extremely brief and simplified summary of the evolution of Nabokov criticism. The Russian émigré criticism (of 'Sirin') and the reviews of Nabokov's earlier works in English tended to focus on his originality and on his literary devices, as did the first book-length studies of the 1960s: the first of these, Page Stegner's *Escape into Aesthetics*, emblematizes this trend in its title.[12] An inevitable division was soon established between commentators equipped to analyse only the English novels (such as Stegner) and those tackling also the Russian texts and source materials (such as Andrew Field). Rather more diverse and specialized studies followed from the 1970s.[13] At the beginning of that decade, the Ardis estate idealized in Nabokov's longest novel *Ada* gave its name to a new publishing house, devoted almost entirely to Russian literature, which was to republish many of Nabokov's works in Russian as well as a number of critical studies on them. The 1980s saw a developing interest in the moral, psychological, and ethical foundations underlying Nabokov's work, a weighing of content as well as form; this decade was also notable for the appearance of detailed monographs on single main works and for important textual and narratological advances.[14] More recently, other-world considerations have become a prominent feature in Nabokov scholarship (as noted above). The 1990s have also seen further synthesized and erudite approaches to Nabokov criticism, a significant renaissance in Russian Nabokov studies[15] (following the publication of his works there, dating from the late Soviet period), and the provision of compendious ancilliary materials (see the note prefacing the Bibliography to this study).

In addition, there are now two Nabokov journals and at least two Nabokov websites.

Finally, a few words should be said about the scope of this study. In a book on this scale it is not, of course, possible to analyse, or even to say something significant about, anything like all of Nabokov's works. A strict selection has had to be implemented, even from among the better known works. Consequently, no treatment is possible here of Nabokov's body of poetry, nor of his plays. Many of the novels not explicated as such have been accorded a passing mention. *Despair* I have written on elsewhere; *Invitation to a Beheading* is receiving widespread critical attention of late.[16] Works I would like to have grappled with, had space allowed, include *The Real Life of Sebastian Knight* and the novella-length novels of the early and the late periods, *The Eye* and *Transparent Things*. There is no analysis as such here of the autobiography *Speak, Memory*, which contains some of Nabokov's most quintessential writing, but some use has been made of this work, particularly in this introductory chapter. I have, though, considered it desirable – indeed, essential – to devote space to Nabokov's critical writings and views and to his rich corpus of short stories, both of which categories of works, along with *Speak, Memory*, are of vital importance in connection with, or alongside, the more celebrated novels which follow. Nabokov's last completed novel, *Look at the Harlequins!*, which is generally less celebrated than it might be, acts as something in the nature of a final Nabokovian mock index (which might be compared to those in *Pale Fire* and to *Speak, Memory*) to the works that precede it.

15

2

VN: The Critic

A full assessment of Nabokov as critic, in the broad sense of the term, would require an evaluation of his critical writings and published lectures, including his translations and editions, as well as a consideration of the briefer expressions of literary comment found in the letters and interviews. Throwaway as many of these latter utterances may appear, they were invariably carefully prepared and meticulously delivered, by means of copious notes or inscribed index cards. Published interviews and letters to the press were revised and re-edited by Nabokov for the collected volume *Strong Opinions* (1973). We shall here deal mainly with the critical writings and the translations into English.

Nabokov wrote his literary lectures in the 1940s and 1950s, for delivery over an academic career spanning nearly two decades at Wellesley College and Cornell; their publication came only posthumously, and there has been some questioning of the editorial approach adopted in the three volumes that we now have. Further refinements are to be expected in due course. Many critical and scholarly advances have been made since Nabokov penned his lectures; moreover, they were intended for student consumption, and not as academic essays. Former students have described the impact made by the lectures and the style in which they were delivered. The enthusiasm they inspired can be easily imagined and, despite Nabokov's reticence over public speaking, there is plentiful anecdotal evidence of his histrionic lecturing abilities.

Nabokov approached his chosen texts by way of a fresh, no-nonsense close reading. 'Style and structure are the essence of a book; great ideas are hogwash': such was the 'central dogma' to be culled from his courses (*LL* xxiii). Utilitarianism has no place in art; all theory is nonsense; 'it is the style peculiar to this or that individual writer of genius that is alone worth discussion' (*LL* 60). 'Realism', to Nabokov, is a meaningless term: 'all fiction is fiction. All art is deception.... The *isms* go; the *ist* dies; art remains' (*LL* 146, 147). Although he would doubtless dismiss any theoretical influence (one shudders to think of his reaction to poststructuralism, as to political correctness!), Nabokov's approach is closest (though unsystematically so) to his contemporary compatriots, the Russian Formalists. His definitions of 'plot', 'theme', 'structure', and 'style' may be less rigorous (see *LL* 16 n), but he delights, for instance, in his (unacknowledged) appropriation from Shklovsky of the chess term 'knight's move' (*LL* 57–8). His overall purpose, 'to reveal the mechanism of those wonderful toys – literary masterpieces' (*LL* 381), sits well with the overall Formalist purpose (of isolating the 'literary' qualities within literature).

Great novels, to Nabokov, were 'supreme fairy tales' (*LDQ* 1). The texts chosen for Nabokov's world literature course, and now represented as the published *Lectures on Literature*, are Jane Austen's *Mansfield Park* and Dickens's *Bleak House* (both suggested by Edmund Wilson), followed by Flaubert's *Madame Bovary* and an old boyhood favourite of Nabokov's, *The Strange Case of Dr Jekyll and Mr Hyde* (despite Wilson's view of Stevenson as 'second rate'). From the twentieth century Nabokov adds 'The Walk by Swann's Place' (as he called the Proust volume in question), Kafka's *Metamorphosis* (or 'Transformation', as he often called it) and Joyce's *Ulysses*. The last three, along with Bely's novel *Petersburg*, were later named as Nabokov's four masterpieces of the twentieth century (*SO* 57). Selection is by positive discrimination – at least for this course, which is described as 'a kind of detective investigation of the mystery of literary structures' (*LL* facing 1). This volume also includes 'The Art of Literature and Commonsense', one of Nabokov's most revealing non-fictional statements.

Nabokov makes heavy use of quotation and plot summary, of the more insightful variety, with a marked – some would say pedantic – attention to detail. He delights in the minutiae of the wordplay of Dickens, entomological matters in Kafka, and 'synchronicity' in Joyce. Nabokov seems to have revered *Ulysses* more than any other novel except *Anna Karenina* (although his long analysis of this novel is not without its criticisms); however, his attitude to the remaining Joycean *œuvre* was less panegyrical: *Finnegans Wake* is dismissed as 'that petrified superpun' (*LL* 122).[1] The *Ulysses* lecture as here published is in fact distilled from a longer version (published in unedited form as *Lectures on Ulysses: A Facsimile of the Manuscript*). Nabokov saw Flaubert as a vital force in nineteenth-century literature, while the example of Proust to him as a supreme exponent of the art of memory is clear. Kafka, like Gogol, can offer the beauty of 'private nightmares' (*LL* 254). Particularly striking in the lectures are Nabokov's concerns with exact dating and with topography. Copious maps and diagrams are reproduced: Jane Austen's England, Joyce's Dublin (in whole and in part), the streets of Combray for Proust, drawings of bugs for Kafka, and even a plan of the layout of the Samsa flat. Students would design a plan of Dr Jekyll's house for Nabokov to annotate. The interrelation of themes and images would be illustrated in diagrammatic form. On the Russian course, even Anna Karenina's sleeping car on the Moscow–Petersburg express is graced with a sketch-plan.

The Russian course (*Lectures on Russian Literature*) consists of Gogol (the only lectures revised by Nabokov for publication, in his celebrated 1944 monograph, which will be discussed below), Turgenev, Dostoevsky, Tolstoy, Chekhov, and Gorky. Also included in the Russian literature volume are an introductory lecture on 'Russian Writers, Censors, and Readers' and minor essays on 'Philistines and Philistinism' and 'The Art of Translation'. Excluded are Pushkin and Lermontov, on whom he wrote elsewhere. These two writers apart, Nabokov had an immense admiration for Tolstoy (though not for *Resurrection* or *The Kreutzer Sonata*), Chekhov, and (in certain measure) Gogol, rather less for Turgenev, and very little for Dostoevsky or Gorky. According to one former student, Nabokov thus graded his Russian writers:

> Tolstoy was A-plus. Pushkin and Chekhov were A. Turgenev A-minus. Gogol was B-minus. And Dostoevsky was C-minus. (Or was he D-plus?) ... 'He who prefers Dostoevsky to Chekhov,' he said, 'will never understand the essentials of Russian life'. (*Q* 37)

For the Russian authors a brief biography is included; the main stress, however, is still on device and style, with scant regard to interpretation. There is no lack, though, of evaluation – or of whimsy. The world of Turgenev, who 'is not a great writer, though a pleasant one' (*LRL* 68), is thus summarized:

> Russia in those days was one huge dream: the masses slept – figuratively; the intellectuals spent sleepless nights – literally – sitting up and talking about things, or just meditating until five in the morning and then going out for a walk. There was a lot of the flinging-oneself-down-on-the-bed-without-undressing-and-sinking-into-a-heavy-slumber stuff, or jumping into one's clothes. Turgenev's maidens are generally good get-uppers, jumping into their crinolines, sprinkling their faces with cold water, and running out as fresh as roses, into the garden, where the inevitable meeting takes place in a bower. (*LRL* 65–6)

Tolstoy is treated with great reverence and at considerable length: *Anna Karenina* – or 'Anna Karenin', as Nabokov always insisted it ought to be in English (*LRL* 137 n) – gets some ninety pages, with detailed notes on Part 1 made towards an unrealized new edition, and even drawings of the heroines' costumes.

More entertainingly, Dostoevsky is subjected to a considerable drubbing – reminiscent of certain of the attacks launched by Russian critics during Nabokov's youth and by Soviet critics later. His characters are all lunatics and neurotics, devoid of any development, whose main purpose lies in 'sinning their way to Jesus' (*LRL* 104). Dostoevsky himself, in Nabokov's view, is essentially a second-rate writer who never got over the influence of European Gothic, mystery, and sentimental novels. This is epitomized in Dostoevsky's 'shoddy literary trick' of assembling in one sentence (in *Crime and Punishment*, 4: 4) the outrageous triangle of 'the murderer', 'the harlot', and 'the eternal book' (*LRL* 110). A gifted writer of scandal scenes (which, Nabokov insists, should be called in English 'rows'), Dostoevsky was potentially a great playwright who 'took the wrong turning and wrote novels' (*LRL* 104). *The Double* was '[t]he very best thing he ever wrote' (ibid.), but this work is never really discussed by Nabokov, while *The Brothers Karamazov*, which, if shorn of Zosima and Alesha, might have been passable, is designated 'a riotous whodunit – in slow motion' (*LRL* 133). Nabokov consistently deprecated Dostoevsky over the years in lectures, letters, and interviews; this did not prevent him, however, from utilizing

Dostoevskian qualities and motifs in his own writing, not least in the creation of his own lunatics and neurotics. The shared biographical parallels – of enforced exile and the murder of the father – Nabokov would not have relished.

Chekhov's gifts, for Nabokov, resided chiefly in the short story rather than the full-length play. In any case, he best exemplifies the 'perfect artist without being exceptionally vivid in his verbal technique or exceptionally preoccupied with the way his sentences curve' ('[w]hen Turgenev', on the other hand, 'sits down to discuss a landscape, you notice that he is concerned with the trouser-crease of his phrase; he crosses his legs with an eye upon the color of his socks') (*LRL* 252). Of Gorky's works, though, in Nabokov's view, there is precious little worth saying beyond the assertion that 'the depths of the good old Russian soul are forcibly conveyed to the reader' (*LRL* 304).

Literature under Soviet socialist realism 'has been limited to illustrating the advertisements of a firm of slave-traders' (*LRL*, facing title-page). Nevertheless, Nabokov tells Edmund Wilson in 1944, he could bring himself to 'select about a dozen readable shorts' for a possible anthology of Soviet fiction (*N–W* 122). Most consistently mentioned with approval in this period was Iurii Olesha, an exact contemporary with a recognizably similar aesthetic approach to Nabokov. Pasternak received Nabokov's approbation as a poet, but certainly not as the author of *Doctor Zhivago* (a novel which was to rival *Lolita* on the best-selling lists in the late 1950s). Neither – predictably – was he fond of the novels of Solzhenitsyn. 'Russian literature of the Soviet period is purity itself', he observed. 'One cannot imagine a Russian writing, for example, *Lady Chatterley's Lover*' (*LRL* 4); not surprisingly, Nabokov could not foresee the prose works of the Third Wave of the Russian emigration, let alone the 'alternative prose' of the *glasnost*' and post-Soviet period. A late flicker of admiration was expressed in 1976, however, for Sasha Sokolov's 'enchanting, touching and tragic book' *School for Fools* (*SL* 560). Essentially, though, for Nabokov, Russian prose is 'all contained in the amphora of one round century – with an additional little cream jug provided for whatever surplus may have accumulated since' (*LRL* 1–2).

While Nabokov may not be the most consistently reliable historian of Russian literature, even within his chronological

limitations, his writings are filled with incisive insights, strong –
if idiosyncratic – opinions, and colourful phraseology. One
would strongly urge students to read Nabokov's critical
writings, although one might never urge students to read *only*
Nabokov. Even on the writers whom he quirkily or (in the view
of many) unjustly lambasts – such as Dostoevsky – Nabokov is
well worth reading, and his criticism provides a refreshing
antidote to the customary pieties and pomposities of the more
pedestrian varieties of academic discourse.

Don Quixote was not a text on which Nabokov chose to lecture; it
was required study at Harvard when he accepted a visiting
appointment there in 1952 (standing in for Harry Levin). The
Lectures on Don Quixote were specially written for this course.
Nabokov gave somewhat grudging credit to what he described
as 'the most scarecrow masterpiece among masterpieces' (*LDQ*
27). He dismisses any claims that *Don Quixote* may be 'the
greatest novel ever written' as 'nonsense'; it is saved only by its
hero, 'whose personality is a stroke of genius on the part of
Cervantes': 'a gaunt giant on a lean nag' (*LDQ* 27–8). Nabokov
details Don Quixote's progress (in terms of victories and
defeats) by a novel method of tennis scoring, according to
which he maintains the final score to be 20–20, or two sets all:
'the fifth set will never be played; Death cancels the match' (*LDQ*
110). This outcome, if the accuracy of Nabokov's computations
may be accepted, reflects 'the harmonizing intuition of the
artist' in 'what seems such a disjointed haphazard book' (ibid.).
By the end of the novel, and over the centuries, Cervantes's hero
has achieved genuine cultural stature and 'the parody has
become a paragon' (*LDQ* 112). Nevertheless, in a later interview
he still relished 'with delight' having torn apart that 'cruel and
crude old book, before six hundred students in Memorial Hall,
much to the horror and embarrassment of some of my more
conservative colleagues' (*SO* 103).
    Nabokov regarded Shakespeare and Tolstoy as supreme
artists, but he preferred to deny the influence of anyone on
his own writing. For instance, he averred 'James Joyce has not
influenced me in any manner whatsoever' (*SO* 102). Many
boyhood favourites he later claimed to have outgrown. One,
though, for whom he retained 'the deepest admiration' was

21

H. G. Wells (*SO* 175). Of modern authors he expressed approval for Borges, Beckett (though for the novels rather than the plays), and Robbe-Grillet. The list of writers he considered 'puffed up' is a long one: 'Camus, Lorca, Kazantzakis, D. H. Lawrence, Thomas Mann, Thomas Wolfe, and literally hundreds of other "great" second-raters' form one brief list (*SO* 54). Others include Rilke, T. S. Eliot, Pound, and Auden, among modern poets; Stendhal, Balzac, and Zola, 'prized highly' by his father, who were denounced as 'three detestable mediocrities from *my* point of view' (*SM* 138); Brecht and Faulkner. Any comparison with Conrad always rankled, while Henry James was a long-standing irritant, and Sartre a particular *bête noire*. Nabokov admitted (in 1950) to a prejudice 'against all women writers' (*N–W* 241), though he did soon relent over Jane Austen. Needless to say, his relationship with at least some of the foregoing writers was rather more complex than he cared to admit.

Turning to Nabokov's published critical work (translations, scholarly apparatus, and the Gogol monograph), we find, not surprisingly, that this is largely concerned with furnishing suitable representations for the English-speaking world of classic works and figures from Russian literature. Once again, it flows from his pedagogical duties. Nabokov was mostly dissatisfied, if not appalled, by existing translations into English from foreign (and particularly Russian) literature. The only acceptable way forward was to produce his own versions. Most of the Gogol material required at Wellesley, he complained in 1942, was 'so abominably botched that I cannot use it. I need "Inspector General" as I can do nothing with Constance Garnett's dry shit' (*SL* 41). The lack of useable critical material in that period (as well as accurate translations) led to the Gogol volume: 'None but an Irishman should ever try tackling Gogol', he averred (*NG* 38). The European Fiction course at Cornell a few years later led to an even worse, 'completely botched' situation with *Madame Bovary* (*SL* 111–12). Occasionally, though, the boot was on the other foot, as when he dismissed the 'incredibly rubbishy Pasternak "translations" of Shakespeare' (*SL* 289). Nabokov stressed that he was 'frankly homosexual on the subject of translators' (*SL* 41) and in 1958, looking for a possible translator for *Invitation to a Beheading*, rejected the idea of Bernard

Guilbert Guerney (of whose translation of *Dead Souls* he *had* approved) and of David Magarshack ('whose work is very poor'), while insisting that 'the translator *must not* be a Russian-born lady' (*SL* 258).

Nabokov began, as usual, with Pushkin and added poems by Tiutchev and Lermontov to produce his *Three Russian Poets* collection of 1944; an expanded version appeared in England in 1947. In those days he believed in rhyming translations. Various other translation projects, one in collaboration with Edmund Wilson, and a proposal for an annotated version of *Anna Karenina* fell short of fruition. In the 1930s (the Paul Léon papers have revealed)[2] he had considered translating *Ulysses* into Russian, and in 1950 he even made plans to translate *The Brothers Karamazov* (*SL* 97). The state of play with existing translations of *Eugene Onegin* led Nabokov to tell Wilson, in 1952, 'I am really very eager to turn *E.O.* into English, with all the trappings and thousands of notes' (*N–W* 268); a week later he affirmed confidently: 'The *E.O.* will not take too much of my time and can be quite smoothly combined with other pleasures' (*N–W* 270). It was to be twelve years, three novels, two translations, and a retirement later before the monumental four-volume Bollingen edition, totalling 1200 pages, was to appear.

Before finally publishing his work on *Eugene Onegin*, Nabokov was to bring two other important translation projects to completion: Lermontov's classic novel *A Hero of Our Time* (in collaboration with Dmitri, published in 1958) and the anonymous early epic, *The Song of Igor's Campaign* (1960).

The Nabokovs' translation of *A Hero of Our Time* was in its day – and is still (having been returned to print in both Britain and North America in the 1980s) – the most accurate rendition of that novel into English, and vastly superior to its several unsatisfactory predecessors. Some readers may find subsequent versions to be more readable. Nabokov's method, for some of his larger projects at least, was to use an earlier English translation as a base; in this case the choice may have fallen on the Moscow-published version by Martin Parker that had first appeared in 1947, and from which conceivably some residual phraseology may survive.[3] Nabokov *père* collaborated on, completed, and polished Dmitri's draft, adding an excellent set of notes and a valuable twelve-page Foreword. There have even been suggestions that the edition as a whole transforms Lermontov's text into a Nabokovian one. His lyric translations apart, Nabokov had also published an article, 'The Lermontov Mirage' (*The Russian Review*, 1941), and it appears that there may have been unpreserved lecture notes. In terms of Nabokov's self-prepared scholarly publications, material on Lermontov in total ranks third in length, behind Pushkin and Gogol. Nabokov, himself a product of Russian literature's Silver Age, was demonstrably, therefore, at greatest pains to guide his adopted readership through Russia's Golden Age.

Again for Cornell teaching purposes in 1948, he found himself needing to make his own working translation of the *Slovo o Polku Igoreve*, the Russian medieval heroic narrative poem which he subsequently decided to call *The Song* (rather than the 'Discourse') *of Igor's Campaign*. A first version, completed by 1952, was revised and annotated throughout the 1950s. By this time Nabokov was adopting a more literal policy towards translation, considering that critical commentary would compensate for poetic loss. As always, though, the final product has been observed to be not without elements of Nabokov's own mannerisms of style. Over this period a controversy had raged as to the genuine medieval provenance of *The Song* (its only manuscript copy having perished in the fire of Moscow during the Napoleonic campaign of 1812). While tending to favour arguments that the work was genuine, Nabokov pressed this stance less for the reasons of patriotic authenticity advanced by Roman Jakobson and much more on behalf of what was to him the far more important matter of artistic authenticity.

Pushkin had always been a supremely important literary figure at many levels for Nabokov: 'the greatest poet of his time (and perhaps of all time, excepting Shakespeare)' (*NG* 29). In 1937 he published an essay on him, in French in Paris, which included verse translations into that language. Pushkin was, naturally enough, a lurking presence in much of Nabokov's fiction, particularly in *The Gift* (for all that Chernyshevsky was the chosen subject for the embedded fictional biography). When Nabokov embarked on his teaching programme in the United States, Pushkin – and versions of his works in English – inevitably loomed large; at Cornell, Nabokov taught Russian literature in the original, as well as in translation. Pushkin was a prominent theme of Nabokov's correspondence with Edmund Wilson, from 1940 until their final falling out – over Pushkin! From the 'little tragedy' of *Mozart and Salieri* and various lyrics in the 1940s, Nabokov graduated to serious work on *Eugene Onegin* by the 1950s.

What *Onegin* needed, in Nabokov's view, was a new kind of translation with copious annotation and commentary. His translation policy for poetry, at this stage, moved strongly away from 'free' rhyme in the direction of literalness. Not only did his theory become more extreme in this respect, contradicting his earlier translation practice (compared with his published Pushkin versions and his first attempts at *Onegin* fragments), but it never quite matched – and probably could not have matched – even his own eventual finished product. Nabokov considered *Eugene Onegin* to be a great world classic, and hoped that a major scholarly edition of Pushkin's 'novel in verse' would establish genuine cultural status for it in the English speaking world. To a certain extent this has happened, but, although a (slightly reduced) paperback impression in two volumes of the revised version did appear in 1975, no single-volume 'popular' edition of the translation, with minimal, or at least greatly abridged, critical apparatus has yet been published.

Were such a printing to take place, its commercial prospects, in competition with the several new or revised versions of *Onegin* in English to have appeared since – all following translating methods of which Nabokov disapproved – might not be too glittering. Even while Nabokov was awaiting publication – and greatly to his annoyance – Walter Arndt's new rhymed translation appeared in 1963. Several others have followed and at least four offerings are currently in print. Nabokov's painstaking rendition, considered by many to be almost unreadable in view of its preference for rare and archaic English expression, despite (or at times even because of) its attempts to retain something of the poetic rhythm of the original, is really at its most usable as a crib to those with some knowledge of Russian (and with a stout English dictionary to hand!). Nabokov uses extreme English rarities, even on occasions when Pushkin had used a common Russian word and without necessarily giving an explanation in his commentary. Nabokov's version did not appear, as he had intended, either in interlinear form, beneath Pushkin's original, or *en regard* (as he termed it: on facing pages). It has been suggested that publication together with stressed interlinear and transliterated Russian would transform the reputation of its creator's 'Nabspeak'.[4] Alternatively, it serves as an invaluable benchmark for those with sufficient dedication to approach their study of Pushkin's text through a plurality of translations (no doubt the best policy, in any event, for those possessed of insufficient, or non-existent, linguistic competence).

Some find that vestiges of the poetic image of the original do still come through Nabokov's version and that it possesses a peculiar defamiliarizing quality of its own – even that, as a totality, the Pushkin work has been absorbed into, or taken over by, a Nabokovian text. On occasions, even, it actually – or almost – works, forming tantalizing flashes of what Alexander Dolinin perceives to be 'like the actual fragments of the virtual ideal translation never to be attained' (*GCVN* 124): a pedantic, but at times brilliant, failure. Its vast commentary (which makes up by far the greater part), perhaps deliberately stronger on Pushkin's West European sources than his Slavic ones, is as full of insights as of pedantry and irrelevance. In academic circles, its literal method, the tone of its commentary, Nabokov's 'strong opinions', his combative attitude to translation and to other translators, and the very size of the edition all combined to make it, if anything, more controversial even than *Lolita*; moreover, it finally killed off Nabokov's friendship with Edmund Wilson.

It may be appropriate to end this chapter with a discussion of Nabokov's single critical monograph, *Nikolai Gogol*, written in English in 1942–3, and seemingly the first book on Gogol to appear in English.

Nabokov's study of Gogol is of modest length (some 40,000 words) and it may come as no surprise to find that it is possessed of quirks sufficient to qualify it as a Nabokovian text in the broader sense: 'the gogolized Nabokov going on to nabokovize Gogol' is Donald Fanger's verdict (*GCVN* 426). It cannot be called a scholarly study, in so far as it lacks footnotes and bibliography: 'I disagree with the bulk of Russian critics of Gogol and use no sources except Gogol himself', Nabokov wrote to his publisher in 1942 (*SL* 41), exaggerating only slightly.

Andrey Bely is the only critic referred to in the body of the text, with the exception of the nineteenth-century radicals whom Nabokov castigates for the folly of their socio-political readings (D. S. Mirsky and the biographer Veressaiev [*sic*] are cited fleetingly in the appendices). Unattributed nods or dismissals along the lines of 'One biographer has even asserted' (*NG* 25) are the preferred style. Neither is it a biography in the sense normally understood, although Oxford University Press thought fit to reissue it in a biographical series in 1985. Nabokov, as he goes along, calls it 'these notes'; much later he referred to it as that 'innocent and rather superficial little sketch of [Gogol's] life' (*SO* 156). 'The best part of a writer's biography is not the record of his adventures but the story of his style,' Nabokov told one interviewer (*SO* 154–5; repeated in the 'Introduction' to *Mary*, 10); it is only in this sense that *Nikolai Gogol* may be considered a biography.

Only three works are treated in any detail: *The Government Inspector* (sometimes known as 'The Inspector General', and inspirationally dubbed 'The Government Specter' by Nabokov), *Dead Souls* and 'The Overcoat' (considered by Nabokov '[t]he greatest Russian short story ever written': *LRL* 317). Several other works are discussed, but only briefly; others still are dismissed or ignored. The book, having opened with Gogol's grotesque death (self-starved and bled with leeches by medics of antediluvian incompetence), proceeds only roughly chrono-logically, concluding, indeed, with his birth (*NG* 150); the main text is then followed with what appears to be a spoof interview with the publisher (entitled 'Commentaries'), a 'Chronology' (purportedly in response to the requirements raised in 'Commentaries'), and an eccentric Nabokov index (dropped in 1973); the 1961 edition then includes an author's biographical note (updated to post-*Lolita* days) and an advertisement for 'two novels by Vladimir Nabokov in New Directions hardbound editions': *Laughter in the Dark* (a reissue of the 1938 English version) and *The Real Life of Sebastian Knight*.

Nabokov's great enthusiasm for Gogol was one of recognized affinities and stylistic delight rather than total admiration. He listed for an interviewer in 1969 the aspects of Gogol that were not to his taste: 'I loathe Gogol's moralistic slant, I am depressed and puzzled by his utter inability to describe young women, I deplore his obsession with religion' (*SO* 156). In 1942 he had told Edmund Wilson how he was 'following Gogol through the dismal maze of his life' (*N–W* 68). His book, which was so strikingly novel to English-speaking readers, amounted to an extended essay in personalized and popularized Russian Formalism; this approach was applied to a 'Gogol' who features as character as much as subject, with 'Nabokov' himself being an assumed authorial pose. Formalism does not normally, of course, concern itself with biography. Nabokov's adaptation, however, sees the fiction and the life as more of a continuum (as with the admixture of memory, autobiography, and imagination in his own prose works): '[Gogol's] being discloses the same quiver and shimmer as does the dream world to which he belongs' (*NG* 142). He homes in on the quirks and the digressions of the Gogolian text (and the Gogolian life): the noses and the devils, the qualities of deception and strangeness, the motifs of flight and travel. He disquisitions on 'poshlust' (his rendition of the Russian *poshlost'*, philistinism, in the form of smug low taste); and he revels in those bizarre '"secondary" dream characters' (*NG* 42), who gain a fleeting mention, often in baroque detail: those denizens of 'this secondary world, bursting as it were through the background' escaping from 'Gogol's true kingdom' (*NG* 52).

In his only published pre-*Eugene Onegin* review of a Nabokov work (*The New Yorker*, 9 September, 1944), Wilson called Nikolai Gogol 'the kind of book which can only be written by one artist about another'. In so far as it stands any comparison at all, its dynamic belletrisme producing penetrating insights into 'the real plots...behind the obvious ones' (*NG* 152) – so seldom found within longer-winded academic studies – it must be with the critical writings of later leading novelists, which it may vaguely resemble in posture and thrust: Milan Kundera's *The Art of the Novel*; the volumes of essays published by such figures as Calvino, Fuentes, Goytisolo, Lem, and Brodsky. Even then, Nabokov's Gogol book is distinct in its attention to a single author. Fanger, a foremost present-day authority on Gogol, calls the study 'brilliant and one-sided' and 'a scintillating primer on anti-realist esthetics' (*GCVN* 421, 426). John Bayley, in 1979, thought it 'the best thing in English written on Gogol' (*Q* 45). In many ways – and certainly in terms of what his book has done for the appreciation of Gogol in the English-speaking world – this must still be true today, while its impact on subsequent Gogol scholarship could command a study in itself.

Another matter again – and one that certainly provides a further justification (were one needed) for the inclusion of this chapter in the present study – is what *Nikolai Gogol*, together with the other critical writings, reveals of Nabokov's own approach to the composition of fiction.

3

VN: Grand Master of the Short Story

The Collected Stories of Vladimir Nabokov (published first as *The Stories of Vladimir Nabokov*, in 1995) comprises sixty-five stories. Four sets of 'Nabokov's dozens' (each containing thirteen works) appeared in four lifetime collections, published from 1958 to 1976. A fifth 'set' – the remainder – are included in *The Collected Stories*, edited by Dmitri Nabokov, and the whole is reordered chronologically.

The make-up of the four 1958–76 'dozens' was part convenience, part selection, and to an extent was arbitrary, with the rediscovery of certain neglected pieces playing a part as well as 'theme, period, atmosphere, uniformity, variety' (*CSVN*, p. xiv). Original publication had in any case involved a variety of stages and locations: Russian émigré periodicals, the three collections published in Russian (two in Europe in the 1930s and a third in New York in 1956); one story written in French ('Mademoiselle O', 1939); and ten stories written in English, placed in American outlets over the 1940s and 1950s. The non-English stories were 'Englished' together with various collaborators (nearly all, in fact, with Dmitri, other than the few early versions made with others). All of these translations had Nabokov's close involvement and have his final authorization as texts. The English stories all appeared in *Nabokov's Dozen* (1958), except for 'The Vane Sisters' (written in 1951, rejected then by *The New Yorker* and first published only in 1959), together with 'Mademoiselle O' and three evidently favoured Russian stories ('Spring in Fialta', 'The Aurelian', and 'Cloud, Castle, Lake'). In the 1970s three further 'dozens' followed, the third of which, *Details of a Sunset and Other Stories*, was called by Nabokov 'the last raisins

30

and petit-beurre toes from the bottom of the barrel' (*SL* 548), although it included several pieces of indisputable value and very considerable Nabokovian interest ('The Return of Chorb', to take just one).

However, 'the bottom of the barrel' had still not been reached. This description was also applied to a preliminary list of nine stories, working towards a final set of thirteen (posthumously attained), which Nabokov had long been planning to 'English' (*CSVN*, p. xvii). One work of those listed, the novella *The Enchanter*, was issued separately in 1986. The remainder have now been assembled and translated by Dmitri (and therefore, technically speaking at least, they lack the final Vladimir Nabokov English imprimatur), along with five other forgotten or unpublished stories, to take their place in what one assumes is intended as the final grand collection. This last thirteen have also appeared as a collection in French and Italian translations.

Many of Nabokov's short stories of the 1920s and 1930s depict scenes of émigré life: the displacement, the longing for the homeland, the lost relationships (with a lover or occasionally a parent), the trauma – and the detail – of adjusting to life in exile.[1] The nearest third-wave émigré equivalent is to be found in the stories and novels of Zinovy Zinik, on whom Nabokov has clearly had a considerable impact. Loss and memory are major themes: the word 'nostalgia' smacks too much of the Nabokovian negative quality of *poshlost'* (see Chapter 2). The typical protagonist, often the narrator, is an exiled Russian of about (or often exactly) Nabokov's age, only sometimes a writer or an intellectual, flooded by memories of a lost love affair. Frequently this protagonist will have a heart condition and/or psychological problems. Triangular love relationships and confrontations with the past (actual or potential) are recurrent features. Frequently West Europeans (usually Germans) take subordinate roles; occasionally they take the lead. Stories may be set against a literary background ('Lips to Lips'); or they may highlight other artistic activities: art, music, the circus ('The Potato Elf') or lepidoptery ('The Aurelian'); cinematic references or imagery are common. The setting of many tales is Berlin (often with flashbacks to Russia); at times it may be elsewhere in Europe, or indeterminate; occasionally it is pre-revolutionary Russia or, in one case ('The Christmas Story'), even Soviet Russia; a few stories are set in England ('La Veneziana', 'The Potato Elf', 'Revenge'). America is the main setting for the English-language stories.

There are stories of a fantastical or fairy-tale nature ('A Nursery Tale', 'The Dragon', 'The Thunderstorm', and 'Wing-stroke'). There are stories in which sadistic violence plays a central part ('The Leonardo', 'Cloud, Castle, Lake', 'Terra Incognita'), which, reduced to mere plot summary, would sound almost like the black miniatures of Nabokov's near-contemporary, Daniil Kharms (the difference being, of course, that Nabokov supplies the context, if not the motivation, for such action). There are even political stories: 'Tyrants Destroyed' is a forerunner of *Bend Sinister*; 'Conversation Piece, 1945' is an attack on both Nazi and Soviet sympathizers in the USA.

Quite a number of these works are clearly experimental efforts towards the elaboration of Nabokov's major theme of exile and lost or abandoned adolescent love, worked through mnemonically and imaginatively in all the forms in which he wrote: letters, poetry, short stories, novels, and on into the triple version of his autobiography (*Conclusive Evidence, Drugie berega,* and finally *Speak, Memory*). They can be seen as a training ground for future, and parallel, novels, as well as serving to develop his outstanding talent for parody. Nabokov rang the permutations on his main thematic patterns in terms of plotline, mood, point of view, and narrative structure. One story ('A Slice of Life') has a female narrator. Female protagonists of great consequence are relatively rare in the prose of the Russian period; not infrequently they are ghostly figures, in that, for one reason or another, they never appear (*Mary*, 'The Return of Chorb', 'Beneficence'). 'A Russian Beauty' and 'Spring in Fialta' may be considered exceptions here, as may the 'stories' published as 'Mademoiselle O' and 'First Love', which ended as chapters of *Speak, Memory*. 'A Bad Day' and 'Orache' are also linked to events described in *Speak, Memory*. 'Ultima Thule' and 'Solus Rex', composed as sections of an uncompleted novel (a casualty of Nabokov's migration – physically from Europe to America, and linguistically from Russian to English), ended as tales approaching novella length.

The less plot a Nabokov story might have, the greater (as a general rule of thumb) its lyrical power: he continued and developed the poetic qualities found in the short prose of his main immediate Russian predecessors in this form, Chekhov and Bunin. He made himself a master both of plotlessness and of the plot twist, and equally of the climactic and the anticlimactic. Atmosphere and observed detail were his compositional hallmarks, both in the miniature (such as 'The Fight') and in the more extended variant ('An Affair of Honor' or 'Spring in Fialta'). Not all his experiments succeeded, but there are among his sixty-five accredited short stories two or three dozen of very considerable artistic merit, and at least a good handful that have strong claims to be acknowledged as masterpieces of the genre.

Detail, angle of vision, optical effects, and modes of perception, in addition to the characteristic epistemological tussling, were striking modernist features in Nabokov's early prose. At the conclusion of 'The Fight', possibly his most accomplished early gem of brevity, the bystanding narrator appears less concerned with the rights and wrongs of the altercation he has just witnessed, and even the 'human pain or joy' caused, than with 'the play of shadow and light on a live body, the harmony of trifles assembled on this particular day, at this particular moment, in a unique and inimitable way' (*CSVN* 146). Observation of effect and the suspicion of a possible mysterious pattern behind the perception of events are of the essence here.

The grouping of unique circumstances, or coincidence (potentially meaningful, if fated only for dissipation), is the situation postulated in 'A Matter of Chance', one of the earliest tales (in *Tyrants Destroyed*). A series of non-encounters, near misses, non-recognitions, and infuriating interventions from the malevolent fates, or agents thereof, all on a long-distance German train, combine to facilitate needless tragedy rather than the alternative of joyful reunion. Finally, the Russian inscription on a lost ring is mistaken for Chinese; consequently the cocaine-snorting protagonist (a certain Luzhin – possibly a distant relation to the chess master of the later *The Luzhin Defense*) suffers semiotic betrayal by his lost Russian alphabet, and the last sign of his wife's unbelievable presence in that very train passes without revelation to anyone other than the omniscient impersonal narrator and, of course, the reader. Fantastic coincidence may occur at any time, but it will be, or will seem, meaningless unless there is at least a minimal awareness of it.

33

Signs and symbols play a vital part in Nabokov's prose: much later he wrote an emblematic story in English with that very title. In his monograph on Gogol (1944), he had declared his intention of writing separately of 'a lunatic who constantly felt that all the parts of the landscape and movements of inanimate objects were a complex code of allusion to his own being, so that the whole universe seemed to him to be conversing about him by means of signs' (*NG* 59). This was to result in the superbly concentrated and enigmatic miniature, 'Signs and Symbols' (1948), regarded by Brian Boyd as 'one of the greatest short stories ever written' (*B Am* 117). Behind, and interwoven within, the surface plot of a displaced ageing Russian Jewish couple, whose son suffers from such a 'referential mania' (*ND* 54), is a tightly interrelating system of imagery that reverberates beyond that story itself and back through Nabokov's earlier Russian fiction. Indeed, for at least one commentator, 'Nabokov's entire career gradually takes on the appearance of an elaborate code with an intricate symbolic meaning.'[2] 'Referential mania', it has been pointed out, 'is a critical disease all readers suffer from': in particular, of course, readers of Nabokov.[3]

'Keys' are a frequently noted motif in Nabokov – sought or mislaid, through into 'Signs and Symbols' (*ND* 55), literally by fictional characters on one level, figuratively by critics on another. 'Everything is a cypher and of everything he is the theme' (*ND* 55) is the diagnosis of the supposed protagonist of 'Signs and Symbols', absent in his incarceration and desperate 'to tear a hole in his world and escape' (*ND* 54). This seems analogous to the final action of Cincinnatus in *Invitation to a Beheading*. In his essay 'The Art of Literature and Commonsense', Nabokov wrote of the madman, 'his personality is beheaded' (*LL* 377). Any attempt at disturbing cosmic monotony is said in 'La Veneziana' to be 'punished, at worst by beheading, at best by a headache' (*CSVN* 105). Beheading is therefore to be linked with madness in Nabokov: an entry to, or from, a world of insanity, as well as a transition to some other possible form of 'otherworld'; it is also, in *Speak, Memory* (85–6), linked to sleep.

'Ultima Thule' is a first-person narrative from an artist named Sineusov, addressed to his recently deceased wife, whom he hopes to somehow contact, perhaps through the agency of his former tutor, Adam Falter, a moribund psychotic who, 'having passed a hygienic evening in a small bordello' (*RB* 148), has stumbled upon a traumatic – and supposedly ultimate – metaphysical discovery. The unwary disclosure of this accidentally acquired 'riddle of the universe' to an Italian psychiatrist had immediately killed the latter with astonishment and Falter (whose name, incidentally, means butterfly in German, in addition to the connotation of its sound in English), fearing a further bout of police meddling, refuses to reveal it to Sineusov. However, shortly before his own death, his obtuse line of casuistic argument in reply to Sineusov's questions is admitted inadvertently to include 'two or three words' constituting 'a fringe of absolute insight' (*RB* 167). Several critics identify echoes in his discourse of the things supposedly best liked by the deceased Mrs Sineusov ('verse, wildflowers and foreign currency': *RB* 153) as the significant words, thus demonstrating her afterlife survival and continued influence.[4] This sounds plausible, but is also open to question, in that this triad seems to stem originally from a 'strange Swede or Dane – or Icelander' (composer of an epic poem, 'Ultima Thule') and that the implied contact with the beyond through a medium scarcely seems a notion as terrifyingly unimaginable as Falter's secret is reputed to be; it could, of course, be a narratorial or authorial plant. Falter's initial exclamation upon hearing Sineusov's demand of 'Well, I'll be damned' (*RB* 156) might also be a candidate (though, once again, damnation – however frightening – hardly sounds original). Completion of the intended novel might or might not have settled such matters but, as it stands, 'Ultima Thule' may be considered Nabokov's counterpart to James's 'The Figure in the Carpet'.

The figure in the carpet of 'The Vane Sisters', Nabokov's later ostensible satire on spiritualism, had to be spelt out to readers in 1959 (having been earlier lost too on the editors of *The New Yorker*, who had rejected it). The last paragraph is revealed to be an acrostic, confirming the posthumous participation of the sisters in the construction of the story, a trick that 'can be tried only once in a thousand years of fiction' (*TD* 201). 'Whether it has come off is another question,' adds Nabokov; the eventual verdict may well be that it has.

Two worlds are a constant postulate in Nabokov's writing, occurring on multiple levels throughout stories and novels: the old and the new, Russia and Europe, East and West, Soviet Russia and America, Russian and English, the living and the dead, this world and another world, reality and memory, actuality and fiction, history and imagination, past and present, material and intangible, diegetic and extra-diegetic. This relish for dualism (or *dvoemirie* as the Russian romantics called it) inevitably looms in any examination of his work. Along with this, and perhaps inextricably connected with it, is the metafictional theme: the text and life, or life as text: 'Again and again she hurriedly appeared in the margins of my life, without influencing in the least its basic text,' the narrator of 'Spring in Fialta' notes of the heroine Nina (*ND* 20). The narrator of 'Ultima Thule' supposes that the detail of this existence might be 'but a muddled preface, and that the main text still lies ahead' (*RB* 166). Added to this is Nabokov's propensity for self-appearance, while the self-conscious aspect (of the fiction as fiction) blends into the intertextual. In Nabokov's work intertextuality consists not only of allusion to literary or other cultural sources, but it goes from tentative beginnings in the short stories to the crescendo reached in his last novel, becoming increasingly auto-intertextual – or, in other words, eventually almost manically self-referential.

As we have begun to see, cross-referencing from work to work illuminates imagery and meaning. That, for instance, sunsets in Nabokov take on a symbolic significance is highlighted by the renaming of the early story 'Katastrofa' (or 'Catastrophe', of 1924) to 'Details of a Sunset' (English version, half a century on), along with the author's claim that this will puzzle readers and infuriate reviewers, while 'corresponding to the thematic background of the story' (*DS* 16). There is a vivid sunset, illuminating the 'architectonic enchantments' (*DS* 23) to Mark as never before when catastrophe has struck. He is granted the heightened vision of the creative artist, which has been building as disaster approaches, at the very moment of fatal accidental impact: this supplies the 'details'.[5] That the 'sunset' should also signify catastrophe (or demise) may already be obvious. Confirmation can, though, be found elsewhere; in one of the first English stories, 'The Assistant Producer' (1943), the 'W. W.' (the White Warriors Union, an extreme and ineffective émigré organization) is termed 'but a sunset behind a cemetery' (*ND* 63). A farcical, if deadly, faction lurks behind a historical disaster.

We now turn in slightly more detail to three stories, all originally written in Russian, to illustrate further aspects of Nabokov's shorter fiction. They will be treated here in reverse chronological order. Most Nabokovian qualities are on view in the quintessential 'Spring in Fialta' (*Vesna v Fial'te*, 1936), one of the three short stories regarded by their author as his best (the others being 'Cloud, Castle Lake' and 'The Vane Sisters'). It may be considered, in a limited sense, a more complex sister-tale to the slightly earlier miniature, 'A Russian Beauty'. The story, which can be seen as synthesizing an existing tradition in Russian short prose while at the same time relating to European modernism,[6] relates a mosaic – in flashback and in foreshadowing – of apparently fortuitous meetings between its narrator Victor and Nina, stretching from Russia in 1917, and – at first at least – 'fraudulently based upon an imaginary amity' (*ND* 13), to the Riviera in the early 1930s, when the situation appears to have intensified.

Victor has speculated that, as a writer, he would 'rely upon memory, that long-drawn sunset shadow of one's personal truth' (*ND* 16). It is the unexpected death of his beloved that releases this mnemonic stimulus. Nina's death in a head-on collision with an approaching circus truck is prefigured by a series of circus signifiers. Similarly, her muse-like role in Victor's artistic birth (he proceeds to the penning of 'Spring in Fialta') is portended in their first scene by a potential (not actual – it being a dark, Russian snow setting – and therefore only figurative) 'wonderful sunburst of kindness' (*ND* 11). The overcast Fialta, by the final moment of parting with Nina, has imperceptibly become 'sun-pervaded throughout' (*ND* 27), as her imminent death (in an 'Icarus': a yellow sports-car that speeds too close to the sun!) will release Victor from Nina – from their 'even more hopeless' intermittent affair and the sunset of their shared Russian past – into an artistic dawn in which imagination is free to enhance memory. Nina had 'a key dangling from her fingers' (*ND* 15) when Victor had chanced upon her on a Paris hotel landing (resulting in perhaps their first full sexual encounter). On a Fialta terrace, scene of their final fortuitous tryst, 'a rusty old key' merely lies at their feet. Fialta, with its old town and its new town and 'fading memory of ancient mosaic design', is an

37

imaginary amalgam, in any case, of 'alto-like' Yalta and Fiume (now Rijeka in Croatia), along with the Russian violet (*fialka*) and an echo of viola (*ND* 7), in which 'past and present are interlaced' (*ND* 22).

It is significant that the explicit 'sun' references to 'sunset' and 'sunburst' noted above were added into the Englished version (first published 1947); the later Nabokov was evidently reinforcing his earlier symbolic patterning. His English style can often be more complex than its earlier Russian counterpart and his vocabulary more recherché. The story is pervaded too with Nabokovian appearances. Both Victor and Ferdinand (the Franco-Hungarian writer husband of Nina) may be seen as some sort of projections of the grand master, although Ferdinand has also been seen as Nina's destroyer[7] and it is 'the plus-foured Englishman of the solid exportable sort' (*ND* 8) who is Nabokov's principal 'representative' in Fialta. All, of course, are somewhat askew with regard to nationality or career (Victor, though a Russian, is a kind of businessman with theatrical interests). It is the Englishman, however, whose glance points Victor towards Nina in Fialta and, apparently bloodthirsty with his 'bright crimson drink' (*ND* 24), he bags 'a compact furry moth' (*ND* 25). Lepidoptery is a sure Nabokovian sign and, although his 'bloodshot desire' is 'in no sense related to Nina' (at least, in Victor's perception: *ND* 24), his bottling of the lepidopteral specimen may be seen as symbolizing the implied authorial dispatching of Nina to whatever her equivalent may be of 'the heavenly fatherland of circus performers' alluded to a little earlier (*ND* 23). It is also reminiscent of another lepidopteral Nabokovian impersonator or representative: the anagrammatic Blavdak Vinomori, who enticed Martha Dreyer to a tango of death nearing the end of *King, Queen, Knave*.

'The Return of Chorb' (1925) was written just after Nabokov's first novel *Mary*, and subsequently achieved prominent status as the title of his first published collection (*Vozvrashchenie Chorba*, Berlin, 1929). This volume, which opens with the title-story, appropriately concludes with 'Terror', a story with which 'The Return of Chorb' has clear affinities. Like 'Spring in Fialta' and

Mary, 'Chorb' provides an example of retrograde plot construction in Nabokov,[8] involving not only regression but the repetition of situations and the reversal of a sequence of events. This should lead to a new beginning on a heightened plane of consciousness; it thus constitutes a spiral, rather than a plain circular form.

Chorb, a 'destitute Russian émigré and *littérateur*' (*DS* 63), has returned to the quiet German city in which he had met and married his wife, a phantom Nabokov heroine who not only cannot appear (other than in retrospect) but remains nameless, except for her family name of Keller ('whom he never named': *DS* 62), being of Germano-Russian parentage. She has in fact died, on honeymoon near Nice, through a bizarre accident, 'having touched, laughing, the live wire of a storm-felled pole' (*DS* 60). Wishing 'to possess his grief all by himself', Chorb has not informed her parents of this disaster. Failing to catch the Kellers at home on his return, he leaves word with the maid that his wife is 'ill' and repairs to the disreputable hotel in which the newlyweds had passed a chaste wedding night. Unable to face the night there alone, Chorb engages the services of a prostitute, on whom he makes no demands. In the early hours, awakening with a cry of terror as he momentarily takes the prostitute to be his restored wife, Chorb frightens the girl away; as she is fleeing the room, the door opens to admit the Kellers, who cannot wait until morning to see their sick daughter. Thereupon, in stunned silence, the story ends. 'The door closed' (*DS* 69); so much for the *fabula*.

Chorb's nocturnal scream may be but a restrained anticipation of that subsequently emitted by Falter in 'Ultima Thule', but it represents the culmination of his eerie odyssey. Without waiting for the funeral, Chorb 'passed in reverse all the spots they had visited together on their honeymoon journey', his purpose thus to recreate 'the near past', so that 'her image would grow immortal and replace her for ever' (*DS* 61). This involves retracing in exactly three weeks the steps of a honeymoon trip which had extended over autumn, winter, and into spring – three seasons – and repeating every action. From Nice, through Switzerland and the Black Forest, to the original 'pacific German city' (*DS* 59), Chorb's arrival at the railway station is followed by a return to the hotel behind the opera house, and indeed the same room as on the first occasion, when he and his bride had escaped there from the family celebrations. Even further retracing is required, as Chorb reports back to her home, 'the familiar house' which he will not enter, only observing the 'amber chasm' of a lighted window: 'a snow-bright sheet' is being spread on a bed (*DS* 65). This may well be the tomb or womb-like bedroom that had been so cloyingly prepared for the young couple, complete with its 'Gothic inscription' which ran '*We are together unto the tomb*' (*DS* 63). Yet 'the very source of his recollections' (*DS* 66) seems rather to be the sordid hotel room; the 'first girl who hailed him', whom he hires to assist in the final perfection of the image, is familiar with the hotel and even with that very room: she recognizes the pink *baigneuse* picture on the wall, and it may well have been a 'lovely blond hair' of hers that the Chorb couple had discovered in the washbasin (*DS* 62–3). Whether, given the ludicrous outcome and the abrupt open-ended closure, Chorb's mission has been satisfactorily accomplished is for the reader to decide.

At a basic level, 'The Return of Chorb' is a black comedy, an urban myth with metaphysical overtones calculated to appeal to Nabokovian sleuths. A moth pings against the light bulb on Chorb's return visit to the hotel room, while leaves, colour, electricity, light, and bulbs are all imbued with symbolic potential. The return of Chorb is a grotesque and obsessional one, while the anticipated (whether by Chorb or by the reader) return of Chorb's wife (unless it be as the moth) fails to materialize. Chorb's ever-laughing wife was killed, or conducted to the beyond, by 'an electric stream' (of sexuality, even? *DS* 60); nocturnal terror at 'her irrational presence' (*DS* 62) is eventually realized with Chorb's climactic scream; the 'white specter of a woman', though, is humanized as the prostitute, wearing only the metaphorical hat of supposed omnipresent spirit, turns on the light (*DS* 69). His eye 'burning with a mad flame' notwithstanding, Chorb considers the ordeal over – at least, until the Kellers walk in! The spiral may lead up to a higher consciousness, or conceivably down to the frozen tableau of speechless farce.

The story may be noted for its symmetry, its expression of anguish, and its sense of classical tragedy (whether serious or burlesque). The test of Orpheus and the quest of Parsifal are fleetingly alluded to in the text (the town boasts a statue of the former and a production of Wagner's opera attended, ironically, by the Kellers) and these appear to be implied in parodic form. Echoes of other myths may also be detectable (the myth of Persephone, which may be a reversal by the *littérateur* Chorb of the myth of Pygmalion). Chorb has returned, seemingly from the underground and without either his Eurydice or the Grail's holy powers of regeneration; and Chorb himself is, in some sense at least, certainly a revenant. Play on the theme of the demon bridegroom (Bürger's *Lenore* and its Russian variants) has also been suggested, as has the most obvious parallel of all – the tales featuring deceased beloveds written by Edgar Allan Poe.[9] The tomb-like bedroom with its Gothic inscription and the motif of the virgin bride, sudden death, longed-for (and possibly actual) return, and immature or equivocal sexuality are all prominent in the fiction (and the biography) of Nabokov's youthful favourite.

'Spring in Fialta' and 'The Return of Chorb' have been singled out previously for critical attention. All but unknown, though, has been 'La Veneziana' (*Venetsianka*, 1924), which for some reason remained unpublished until its French and Italian versions (as title-story of another collection of thirteen) of 1990 and Dmitri Nabokov's English translation of 1995. The original Russian text is only now becoming available. In a rare comment on this then-unpublished work, Boyd writes: 'With colorful characters and well-controlled romantic entanglements, the story reads like Pirandello: clever metaphysical twists, but with none of the nimbus of mysterious meaning the mature Nabokov could imply' (*B Rus* 235). For Dmitri Nabokov, it 'echoes Nabokov's love of painting (to which he intended, as a boy, to dedicate his life) against a backdrop that includes tennis, which he played and described with a special flair' (*CSVN*, p. xvi).

'La Veneziana' is distinctive too for its setting: a castle in rural England, owned by a retired Colonel who collects Old Masters. His son Frank is staying during the summer vacation from university (one might assume Cambridge), with Simpson, a college friend. Also in residence are McGore, a connoisseur, restorer, and procurer of paintings, with his young wife

Maureen. McGore has just obtained a picture known as the *Veneziana*, said to be by the Venetian artist Luciani (known as 'del Piombo'). The Venetian beauty depicted bears an uncanny resemblance to Maureen McGore, with whom Frank has been conducting an affair. Simpson, prompted by McGore, has a vision of merging with the picture in contemplation of the adorable Maureen (or Veneziana). Frank, convinced that Simpson has tipped off the Colonel about their relationship, takes his revenge by adding a quick portrait of Simpson to his father's Venetian canvas, and runs away with Maureen. McGore, who is able to erase Simpson from the picture ('Remarkable. Poor Simpson has disappeared without a trace', declares the Colonel: *CSVN* 113), then admits that the *Veneziana* is but 'a magnificent imitation' (*CSVN* 114) of del Piombo, painted by Frank (who had long nurtured the potent demon of artistic talent), with whom he has shared the 'most sumptuous sum' (*CSVN* 92) paid by the Colonel. The Veneziana retains 'a secretly mocking smile at the corner of her lips' (*CSVN* 115), but the Colonel ends up proud of his son. Frank, however, has the girl and the money and has demonstrated his artistry. In tennis terms, the result is a repeat of the opening match of the story: game, set, and match to Frank and Maureen over the Colonel and Simpson, with McGore left as spectator.

However, surface frivolity and certain imperfections apart, this painterly tall story is in itself artistically composed. As well as representing the 'artistic fantastic' (fiction in which a paranormal relationship is posited between life and a work of art), 'La Veneziana' is constructed from a palette of framings, paintings, and colours. At the same time it is an English society tale of etiquette and intrigue. Portraits are depicted by word as if by brush, featuring fingers and windows as motifs with dexterity and symmetry. The Colonel's desire to coat Maureen with varnish and substitute her for Luciani's canvas is an ironic anticipation of later developments; McGore considers 'life's Creator only a second-rate imitator of the masters whom he had been studying for forty years' (*CSVN* 92). Realized too, in terms of fiction and fantasy, are Simpson's musings on figures descending from the canvas and the 'inverse' action of stepping into a picture (*CSVN* 100). The fantastic level of the tale reaches its climax when Simpson, communing with Maureen/Veneziana, (literally) enters the picture, while Frank paints him onto it; McGore's vision is further realized as Simpson feels himself 'growing into the varnish' and 'growing into the canvas' (*CSVN* 111). The interloping Simpson is wiped from the *Veneziana*: 'the slightly damp paints of which he had consisted' now adhere to McGore's rags and are thrown from the window, as a slumbering Simpson is found in the garden (*CSVN* 113). The 'only riddle of this whole tale' (*CSVN* 114) remains the 'small dark lemon' picked up by the gardener, the same lemon that had been handed to Simpson in the Venetian penumbra, thus leaving this anecdote of the world of art with a vestige of the fantastic.

The allusion to 'mysterious tales about portraits coming to life' (*CSVN* 100) links 'La Veneziana' with antecedents in Russian literature (Gogol and others) and the artistic fantastic in European and Anglo-American fiction (Balzac, Poe, and Hawthorne). However, the closest parallel, in Nabokov's combination of painting with manners in an English country-house setting – though he would have thanked no one for the observation – is with Henry James, an author he is not known to have read until somewhat later. With regard to its place in the Nabokovian *oeuvre*, 'La Veneziana' is interesting as a unique example of a full, if immature, exploration of the painting theme frequently included, in a minor key, in his subsequent fiction (*Glory, The Luzhin Defense, Despair,* and *Laughter in the Dark*); it thus presages some of the more masterly works to come.

4

VN: The Russian Novelist
– *Mary* to *The Gift*

Between 1925 and 1938 Nabokov wrote nine novels in Russian (including, in most counts, the novella, *The Eye*). Of these the first, *Mary*, and the last, *The Gift* (from which he broke off in 1934 to write *Invitation to a Beheading*), may be considered the most 'Russian', in terms of their concern with émigré life (featuring Russian protagonists displaced to a Berlin setting), of their harking back fondly to a lost past in Russia, and their deep concern (at various levels) with Russian culture. The other 'Russian novels' most comparable in these senses may be said to be *The Luzhin Defense* and *Glory*. The former is distinct in its heavy emphasis – literal and symbolic – on the system and patterning of chess, while the latter – in any case more cosmopolitan in its settings – is something rather more of an imaginative pseudo-autobigraphical fairy tale. The shortish *Mary* may be considered Nabokov's overture to his Russian novels, and the full-length *The Gift* his symphonic culmination. Discussion in any detail of the novels in Russian will therefore here be confined to these two works.

When *Mashen'ka* was Englished in 1970, Nabokov seemed to have resolved to call it 'Mariette' (*SL* 459), but eventually settled for *Mary* which, for some reason, or so he finally decided, 'seemed to match best the neutral simplicity of the Russian title name' (*M* 9). Nabokov also acknowledged, in his 1970 'Introduction', a similarity between his own reminiscences (now known to readers through *Speak, Memory*) and those of *Mary*'s protagonist, Ganin, and between Mary herself and his first love, 'Tamara'. He also claims greater faithfulness to the original text (in his collaborative translation with Michael Glenny) than in the versions of 'say *King, Queen, Knave*' (done together with his son). It will come as no surprise that certain (auto)biographical elements in common are to be discerned, not only with *Speak, Memory*, but also with the intervening *The Gift*, a variant (auto)biographical projection, as well as with a number of minor works (for instance, the story 'A Letter that Never Reached Russia').

Mary features a young Russian émigré intellectual (very much of artistic temperament, if not declaredly a writer) named Ganin, living with other Russians in a Berlin rooming-house close to the railway line (trains and railway stations are important in much of Nabokov's Russian fiction). He discovers from a photograph – or at any rate he appears to believe – that the wife of another resident, named Alfyorov, is none other than the Mary with whom he had had a passionate teenage relationship in Russia (as Nabokov had himself experienced with his Tamara – in reality one Valentina Shulgin). Mary is due to arrive in Berlin from Russia in a few days to join her husband, from whom she has been parted for four years. Ganin decides to step in, in place of Alfyorov, whom he helps to inebriate, and take her off to a resumed life together. Instead, at the last moment, he boards a train to France – alone.

The eponymous Mary never appears in the present of the novel, only in Ganin's reminiscences, or ruminations: '[h]e was a god, recreating a world that had perished' (*M* 40). Memory and imagination have by now – if they have not always – fused or blurred into one:

> Now, many years later, he felt that their imaginary meeting and the meeting which took place in reality had blended and merged imperceptibly into one another, since as a living person she was only an uninterrupted continuation of the image which had fore-shadowed her. (*M* 49)

Image, 'poor snapshot' (*M* 34), yet 'exactly as he had remembered her' (*M* 54): does, or did, 'Mary' exist at all? Has she any connection in 'reality' with Alfyorov's wife?[1] The capricious and obsessive Ganin, who consistently prefers fantasy over reality in his practice of the art of memory, is himself something of a mystery, with his two passports and false surname (see *M* 80). Mary, at least in Ganin's yearning imagination, becomes, in Brian

Boyd's words, 'a personalized image of the émigré dream, the hope of reliving and resuming the happiness of remembered Russia' (*B Rus* 245). Ganin's reflections on their sexual past may appear contradictory. Whether she symbolizes the Russian past or the return of the Eternal Feminine (a strong myth of Russia's 'Silver Age'[2]), Ganin fails to confront her. The *pension* inhabitants are a cross-section of the emigration, mostly on the fringes of artistic activity: Ganin has acrobatic abilities; Podtyagin is an aged and ailing poet, trying to get to Paris; there is also a homosexual pair of ballet dancers; Ganin and other émigrés 'shadow' as film extras. Indeed, the boarding house can be seen as itself emblematic of the émigré situation (at more levels than one), as 'a kind of shadow-land, a halfway house between one existence and another'.[3]

Some of these characters make subsequent appearances in other Nabokov works, either as actual, or what can be considered equivalent, figures: Mary potentially equals various Nabokovian – very often phantom – heroines; Ganin, who just may be a pathological liar (like Smurov, of *The Eye*, or Hermann of *Despair*), has many counterparts, at least up to Van Veen of *Ada*, who also walks on his hands. The Alfyorovs as a couple (and Mashenka by name) make fleeting appearances in *The Luzhin Defense*; while *The Gift* includes reference to the dead poet Podtyagin. Blithely, and 'with merciless clarity' (*M* 105), Ganin heads for France, leaving a trail of chaos behind him in émigré Berlin: he abandons two women with feelings towards him (potentially three, if we can count Mary), a drunken Alfyorov, and a dying Podtyagin. Physical reality is rejected in favour of image and memory.

Many of what are to become Nabokov's stock figures, themes, and motifs are now in place within a short novel of artful construction. Not least the epigraph, from Pushkin's *Eugene Onegin*, points forward to the Pushkinian subtext that assumes a greater importance in *The Gift*.

The Gift may be seen in part as a far more mature and larger-scale version of *Mary*, with its added mixture of narrative styles and jumbling of generic forms. Furthermore, it is permeated with a strong 'literary' component, mostly (though not exclusively) relating to Russian literature – in both its nineteenth-century 'classical' and émigré complections. First published (serially as

Dar) in an émigré journal in 1937–8, the work appeared shorn of its fourth chapter, the 'biography' of the nineteenth-century radical critic, Nikolai Chernyshevsky (to give his name in this instance its more standard spelling), which was censored by the editors in circumstances strikingly similar to those pertaining within the novel itself – just as Fyodor experiences publishing difficulties over it. It was published in full in New York in 1952. Even in its truncated form, Nabokov's last Russian novel was considered 'the most original, unusual and interesting piece of prose writing in the entire émigré literature between the wars'.[4] The English version followed eleven years later, by which time Nabokov's reputation as an American novelist had been established and *The Gift* was thrown open to vastly wider scrutiny. *Dar/The Gift* is now frequently classified among the great twentieth-century Russian novels, and is the only Russian-language novel by Nabokov for which such claims are made.

The English edition of *The Gift* (published in 1963 and reissued by Penguin in 1981) presents the non-Russian reader in particular with a number of albeit in most cases minor difficulties or inconveniences. The Russian subject-matter of the novel has caused Nabokov to leave a number of transliterated Russian words or expressions in the text (in addition to the sprinkling of French included too in the original Russian text); these have normally been given as well in translation. Some at least of Nabokov's 'alterations' in translation,[5] with regard to style or vocabulary, add to rather than reduce the text's complexity. His transliteration was never entirely consistent, nor did he adhere to the most customary system: hence the Polish-looking 'Chernyshevski' (rather than ending the name with the most common '-y', or the more accurate '-ii' or '-ij', ending).[6] That writer's novel (*Chto delat'*?) is called in Nabokov's English *What to Do?*, rather than the more standard rendering, *What is to be Done?* (translations under that title, prior to 1963, had appeared dated 1886 and 1961; the additional formulation 'What Are we to Do?' [*G* 275], is of course a deliberate mangling, as part of a spoof review). Zina's mother, Marianna Nikolaevna Shchyogolev, has become (whether by accident or design) almost invariably 'Marianna Nikolavna'. These details remain trivial – indeed, some references to Russian literature are made more explicit in the English edition – but given the plethora of

47

literary and historical allusions in the text it is unfortunate that (unlike the cases of *Lolita* or *Ada*) no annotated edition has appeared (a Russian edition with some annotation was published in Moscow in 1990). Critical studies apart, the English reader of this intricate work has to get by just with the aid of Nabokov's two-page – and, as usual, idiosyncratic – 'Foreword' from Montreux.

Nabokov complained, rather perversely perhaps, that Henry James failed to prove in *The Aspern Papers* 'that Aspern was a fine poet' (*N–W* 53). He makes no such omission in the case of his own literary heroes, from Fyodor Godunov-Cherdyntsev of *The Gift* to John Shade in *Pale Fire*. Furthermore, *The Gift* can be said to a considerable extent to be made up of books within a book: works of literary apprenticeship, or a 'training programme' (*G* 94), framed by an émigré love story and set in Berlin from 1926 to 1929. Whereas in *Mary* the mood of reminiscence seems to take precedence over experiencing the present, in *The Gift* the present, the past, and artistic imagination seem to be accorded greater equality in value, as the themes of Nabokov's Russian fiction aspire to their fullest consummation.

Chapter 1 includes examples of Fyodor's early verse compositions; it dwells on these attempts to recreate details from his Russian childhood, on the interaction between memory and imagination, and the process of poetic inspiration. Pushkin is the guiding force; this chapter, among other things, represents the lyric phase in the career of the budding artist and reflects that of his literary godfather. Unlike the gems of the latter, however, Fyodor's lyrical work does not produce poetry of any great genius. Still under the impact of 'the purest sound from Pushkin's tuning fork' (*G* 93), Fyodor follows his artistic mentor into prose in Chapter 2. Inspired by Pushkin's Caucasian travelogue, *The Journey to Arzrum*, Fyodor plans a biography of his father, Konstantin Godunov-Cherdyntsev, a noted explorer and naturalist who had failed to return from his last expedition and is presumed to have perished amid the chaos of civil war. Fyodor's much-loved and long-since missing biological father had himself been imbued with a Pushkinian spirit. Copious researches for this project of biographical reminiscence are undertaken by Fyodor, but he finally abandons it as his own subjective and creative fantasies come to dominate the parental portrayal.

In Chapter 3 Fyodor moves as though 'from Pushkin Avenue to Gogol Street' (*G* 136) and takes the seemingly unlikely decision to write a biography of the beacon of materialist aesthetics and revolutionary martyr, N. G. Chernyshevsky (seen by many as the original godfather of socialist realism): this extended essay is given verbatim as Chapter 4. The Gogolian slant is rather more of a stylistic 'knight's move' than a thematic shift, for Pushkin himself had become ever more involved with historical research towards the end of his career (having earlier begun a biography of his own Ethiopian ancestor: *The Blackamoor of Peter the Great*). The anti-hagiographic tone of 'The Life of Chernyshevski' stems not only from the pointing up of diametrically opposed aesthetic differences, but from its avowed composition 'on the very brink of parody', reminiscent of 'those idiotic "*biographies romancées*" where Byron is coolly slipped a dream extracted from one of his own poems' (*G* 184). In addition, it shares rich interconnections in terms of thematics, structuring, patterning, and imagery with the surrounding layers of the novel. While treated, both within the novel and outside it in the émigré literary world, as a 'genuine' (if frequently perceived as vicious) literary biography, and based on close usage of actual primary and secondary sources (apart, that is, from 'his best biographer', Strannoliubski, or 'Strangelove': *G* 202),[7] Fyodor's composition belongs firmly within the totality of *The Gift*; it is worth stressing that Nabokov never sought to publish or republish it as an independent 'critical biography'. 'The Life of Chernyshevski' is to be regarded solely as the posed opus of Fyodor.

The novel that Fyodor plans to write, in Chapter 5, is frequently taken to be what we now know as *The Gift*, although this in itself remains a point of contention.[8] Moreover, the text is replete with further mini-works, tales, fragments, quotations from varied sources, and supposed or intended works. Not least, Fyodor plans to translate a philosophical work by the fictitious French philosopher Delalande. These factors all contribute to the polyphonic quality (in a wider sense) of *The Gift*.[9] First-time readers (and Nabokov would like to insist on re-reading as essential to any meaningful interpretive process) may be instantly confused by alternations in first-person and third-person narration and by rapid switches in point of view. Sentences can be long, and paragraphs may on occasion extend for pages. The main narrative constantly mixes with rumination or stream of consciousness, quotation and analysis of the protagonist's poems, and sundry further interpolated items of discourse.

In Chapter 1 we are given examples of Fyodor's poems, accompanied by recollections, commentary, and possible material from the imagined review. Following this comes a description of the poetry of the deceased Yasha Chernyshevski (less favourably evaluated by Fyodor). Alexander Chernyshevski, Yasha's father, suggests that Fyodor might describe the life, 'in the form of a *biographie romancée*', of Nikolay Chernyshevski, 'our great man of the sixties' (G 43); despite saying it 'on numerous occasions' (ibid.), Alexander seems to have forgotten this when Fyodor announces his intention 'about three years' later 'of getting down to it' (Chapter 3: G 181), and the 'biography' takes up Chapter 4. At the same time, Yasha's mother 'persistently counselled' Fyodor to write about her son (G 43); this story, we are told, 'remained unused by the writer' (G 44), although it follows immediately in the text of *The Gift* (44–53). Similarly, much of the 'unrealized' study of Fyodor's father is included in Chapter 3. Chapter 1 proceeds to show poetic inspiration at work on Fyodor, leading to a new poem beginning 'Thank you, my land' (quoted G 58). A semi-farcical literary evening is dominated by an account, with quotations, of the reading of an inept 'philosophical tragedy' by a Baltic Russian writer named Busch; there then follows what turns out to be an imagined conversation spanning a century of Russian literature, supposedly on the way home, between Fyodor and a fellow-émigré poet and kindred spirit named Koncheyev.

In Chapter 5 – following a survey of the reviews of his Chernyshevski biography, another farcical literary gathering, the development of his amorous relationship with Zina Mertz, and a further imagined discussion with Koncheyev – Fyodor threatens to write 'a classical novel, with "types", love, fate, conversations' (G 318); his own autobiographical material, fit for a novel, must first mature in content and style, and be shuffled and twisted until 'nothing remains of the autobiography but dust' (G 332). Such a reworking might eventually result in a text something like *The Gift*. The foibles of Fyodor as author may correspond to such a pattern; those of Nabokov as grand-*auctor* certainly do.

Submerged patternings of time and fate, quietly ongoing as the book unfolds, are revealed in part in the later stages and recognized within the text by Fyodor; other such connections are apparent only to the more astute first-time reader; still others only to the re-reading reader. The same applies to correspondences and clusters of motifs and 'types' (often in threes or triangles) scattered across the component parts of this apparently heterogeneous texture of *The Gift*; these may be presented in serious or parodic form.

Fyodor, Yasha Chernyshevski, and Nikolay Chernyshevski feature prominently in sections of the text as budding writers and biographical subjects; biography, indeed, is important in relation to Konstantin Godunov-Cherdyntsev, Nikolay Chernyshevski, and Fyodor himself. Father-and-son relationships are vital in the cases of Konstantin Godunov-Cherdyntsev and Fyodor; Alexander Chernyshevski and Yasha (in these two instances there seems to be both an actual and a spectral relationship); and Nikolay Chernyshevski and son Sasha; the 'relationship' between the two sets of Chernyshevskis is in itself a parodic one. A further trio of female muse figures (whether girlfriend, fiancée, or wife) crossing the three levels of plot can be assembled in the personae of Zina Mertz, Olia G., and Olga Sokratovna – the respective partners (or would-be partners) of Fyodor, Yasha, and Nikolay Chernyshevski. Yasha, Olia, and Rudolf form one sexual 'triangle inscribed in a circle' (*G* 45). Nikolay, Olga Sokratovna, and Dobrolyubov (or various substitutes) may be said to represent another (parodically reminiscent, too, at further removes, of the triangular situation of *What is to be Done?* and of the fatal triangle at the end of Pushkin's life). Imparted through the wisdom of Strannolyubski is an indication of a 'circumference controlling all life of the mind' that lurks concealed in the Hegelian triad (*G* 224), especially as operated by Chernyshevski.

In a similar vein the motif of travel extends over the component chapters. Fyodor has himself travelled into exile and continues to voyage widely, at least in his imagination, accompanying the subjects of his biographical projects to Asia and Siberia. Konstantin Godunov-Cherdyntsev's intrepid expeditions of exploration and lepidopteral research are paralleled by Nikolay Chernyshevski's travels and travails in Siberia –

again in exile. Fyodor's mother makes an impetuous and abortive journey to surprise her husband; Olga Sokratovna makes an even more farcical expedition briefly to join her husband in Siberia (a journey that in itself parodies the exploits of the Decembrist wives under the yoke of Nicholas I). The 'theme of "travelling"' is, moreover, overtly pointed up near the beginning of the Chernyshevski biography (G 198).

Critical and aesthetic debate is another recurrent category of discourse. The impact of Pushkin operates on Konstantin, as well as on Fyodor, and provides a challenge too to Nikolay Chernyshevski. In addition to matters of poetics and prosody, perception – of both natural and man-made worlds – is a constant concern, while political repression and forms of incarceration (as well as exile, noted already above) feature at various levels. Death, as ever in Nabokov, interposes on all strands of the novel, as do varied dealings with a putative spirit world. A final trio of Nabokovian literary self-projections comprises: Fyodor (who shares somewhat distorted biographical traits with his creator), the poet Koncheyev (included as an *alter ego*, to engage in fictitious dialogues with Fyodor), and a figure named Vladimirov (whose description and literary profile resemble Nabokov's and who appears at the writers' meeting); in Chapter 5 the three are overtly grouped in a single sentence (G 292–3). Many further motifs and images could be indicated (some of which will emerge from the ensuing analysis of the opening pages of the novel). Just two trivial details of what Karlinsky called 'symmetry and recapitulation'[10] will be added now: the reports of 'insanity' in Denmark (G 61) are balanced in the final chapter by that country's reappearance as destination for the departing Shchyogolevs (the mother and stepfather of Zina Mertz); and the architect Stockschmeisser (with dog), on the scene at the time of Yasha's suicide, reappears in the same vicinity years later when a small plane has crashed (see G 51 and 302).

A detailed analysis of *The Gift* would require a (still-awaited) monograph in itself. For present purposes we shall return (and, naturally enough, not without the benefit of hindsight) to see what is revealed in the opening ten pages of Chapter 1.

The epigraph (purportedly quoted from something called *A Textbook of Russian Grammar*) establishes nature, Russia, and mortality as preoccupations to come, and may be said to balance the thoughts quoted later from the invented French thinker, Pierre Delalande. The novel proper commences with removals into a Berlin boarding-house, which is in fact a double move. The couple receiving their furniture from a removal van are described first; in Gogolian style, the narrative concentrates initially on characters who will play little or no part in the action to follow. The other new tenant is the first-person narrator, with just a suitcase, containing 'more manuscripts than shirts' (G 11). The second paragraph begins: 'Some day, he thought, I must use such a scene to start a good thick old-fashioned novel' (ibid.); the abrupt switch to third-person narration almost distracts from the ironic fact that a good thick (if not old-fashioned) novel has just started with this very scene. Observation of city detail immediately rubs shoulders with metafictional quirk: 'somebody within him, on his behalf, independently from him, had absorbed all this, recorded it, and filed it away' (ibid.). This leads Julian Connolly to discern a 'fundamental bifurcation of identity' between authorial and character elements of the narrator, Fyodor.[11]

The minutiae of urban landscape, together with infiltrations from the natural world, with an emphasis on angles, surfaces and reflections, and colours and tastes, develop into interior monologue on 'architectural detail that effusively caught one's attention' (G 12); conjecture over a hidden counterpoint in the siting of Berlin stores gives way to annoyance at the false *politesse* that surrounds transactions with shopkeepers. However, even this compensates with 'that extra little payment in kind' (G 13), in the form of observed detail with potential for future artistic use. Fyodor suddenly remembers that 'my collection of poems has been published' (a first-person interpolation: G 14). His German landlady (with the strangely Russian-sounding name of Frau Stoboy) has left his keys in his room; keys, an important motif for the novel,[12] receive a first mention, as the exterior (of the street) gives way to the interior (of the room, and the view from it). The desire 'to transform the wallpaper (pale yellow, with bluish tulips) into a distant steppe' (G 15) anticipates Russia and the travels of Fyodor's father, as does 'the desert of the desk' and the armchair that has to 'become suitable for travelling' (ibid.).

The literary subtext (already indicated by the poetry collection and the 'first rhymes' to sprout from the desk) is vitalized by a phone call from Alexander Chernyshevski (who in himself prefigures the future Chernyshevskian layers), with news of a favourable review (in fact, merely an April-fool joke) and inviting Fyodor over to see it at one of his literary gatherings that evening (heralding scenes of émigré literary life). Fyodor, in his rapture, wants to compliment Frau Stoboy on her 'pale yellow dress with bluish tulips' (transposed from the wallpaper?), and her 'George Sandesque regality', but 'with a beaming smile... nearly tripped over the tiger stripes which had not kept up with the cat as it jumped aside' (G 16). Not only 'a few hundred [émigré] lovers of literature', but eventually – from 1963 on – an English readership too 'would... appreciate his gift' (ibid.). Nabokov's vivid imagery underscores the first reference to Fyodor's 'gift'.[13] What follows then is excerpts from the imagined review (-cum- 'internal review') of the fifty-poem collection on the theme of childhood. '[T]he flesh of poetry and the spectre of translucent prose' (ibid.) are to be transposed as Fyodor's artistic career progresses into, we might say, the flesh of prose with the spectre of translucent poetry, Nabokov wishing, as always, to minimize – or indeed abolish – any distinction between them. 'Now he read in three dimensions' (G 17); this piece of information serves as an inspiration to Nabokov's ideal readers, reconstructing the memory and the imagination that combined to produce the sequence of poems in question. The opening one of these, 'The Lost Ball', is then given in its full twelve lines.

Recollection of light and shadow, darkness and bedtime, leads to an analytical and inspirational process of reverie into early memory. Darkness anticipates 'the darkness to come', a turning of life 'upside down so that birth becomes death' (G 18). Such musing on artistic responses to death provides a first tentative fulfilment of the hint in the epigraph, foreshadowing later rumination of this type in the novel (including the thoughts of Delalande) and corresponding to similar lucubrations found throughout Nabokov's œuvre: according to the opening sentence of Speak, Memory, for instance, 'common sense tells us that our existence is but a brief crack of light between two eternities of darkness' (SM 17). There then follows (auto)biographical reminiscence on the Godunov-Cherdyntsevs' estate and their family life in Russia. Significantly here, between poems and verse fragments, there appears a list of exotic objects that Fyodor's father 'somehow happened to bring back from his fabulous travels' and a mention of his butterfly collection, while 'a special intuition forewarned the young author that some day he would want to speak in quite another way…about his famous father' (*G* 21). The Pushkinian move in the direction of prose (biography and history) is thereby announced.[14] The one missing ingredient of importance from what is to come is the theme of love; this begins to emerge somewhat obliquely only later in the chapter.

The Gift is, among other things, a novel of romance between Fyodor and Zina Mertz, his (second) landlady's daughter. Characters in Nabokov are frequently introduced, or alluded to, before any relevance they may have to the work as a whole is clear. Zina Mertz is mentioned to Fyodor (*G* 60) by the painter Romanov among the adherents of Margarita Lorentz's artistic soirées; there is a hidden reference to her a little later, as 'a Russian girl in their office', requiring assistance with legal translations (*G* 70). As Fyodor dislikes Romanov, Madame Lorentz, and the lawyer in question, he passes up what could have been much earlier opportunities to get acquainted with Zina. She is mentioned again as 'a daughter from the first marriage' (*G* 133) when Fyodor is considering moving his lodging to 15 Agamemnonstrasse; even then he takes an instant dislike to Shchyogolev and the room, only changing his mind when he spots a short, pale-bluish, gauze dress across an armchair in the dining room (*G* 135), presumably on the assumption that this might promise future *frissons*. The baring of this device, as the manipulations of fate, occurs overtly at the very end of the novel; ironically too the dress was not even Zina's: 'it was my cousin Raissa's – she's very nice but a perfect fright' (*G* 331). The relationship develops from Chapter 3. 'What shall I call you? Half-Mnemo*syne*? There's a half shim*mer* in your surname too' (*G* 146); the sonic effect is even closer (to 'Zina Mertz') in the Russian original (*Mnemozina: mertsanie*). Fyodor bursts into rhyming prose to celebrate his 'half-fantasy' and muse. Zina had bought a copy of Fyodor's poetry two years before, had collected clippings of his verses in the émigré press, and suddenly, albeit briefly, emerges as the addressee of his prose, as 'you' (*G* 140), in the manner of Véra Nabokov (as at the end of *Speak, Memory*).

The Gift, then, is a love story, as well as a literary *Bildungsroman* (or *Künstlerroman*): a portrait of the artist as a young man. It is also a city novel, in the European modernist tradition set by Andrei Bely's *Petersburg*, Joyce's *Ulysses*, and Döblin's *Berlin Alexanderplatz* (the first two of which Nabokov greatly admired). Like the protagonists of those city novels, Fyodor spends much of his time walking the city streets and environs; in his case, recollecting Russia and his childhood, 'straight from the hothouse paradise of the past, he stepped onto a Berlin tramcar' (*G* 79).[15] The modernist epistemological preoccupation in *The Gift*, as in much of Nabokov's work, brushes against the 'ontological flickers' more characteristic of postmodernism, the glimpses of 'the unusual lining' of life (*G* 169), or perhaps beyond. The overall structure of this central novel (in more senses than one) of Nabokov's *œuvre* has been variously discerned as circular, as folding back under itself to form a Möbius strip, and as a receding spiral.[16] As well as demonstrating the mature accomplishments of Nabokov's prose in Russian and, a quarter of a century later, reconfirming the Janus-faced pinnacle of his pre-war novelistic prowess to an English readership, its literary purpose can be held additionally to be twofold: the turning, finally, of the phenomenon of exile to artistic advantage; and a masterly exhibition of the art(s) of fictionalized autobiography and creative biography.[17] The final irony of the latter exercise, as pointed out by Connolly,[18] is not only the transformation of Nikolay Chernyshevski's career, perceived as a mawkish saga of monumental ineptitude (on the part of hero and authorities alike), into a work of art, but also the framing, or imprisoning, of this composition within 'the shape of a ring, closed with the clasp of an apocryphal sonnet' (*G* 188) – one presented, what is more, back to front.[19] This device is only topped by the Pushkinesque final paragraph of *The Gift*: the final point to the *Eugene Onegin* pointer (signalled as far back as the epigraph to *Mary*) is the *Onegin* stanza presented in prose – which is effectively to mark Nabokov's farewell to the Russian novel.

5

The *Lolita* Phenomenon

What is here termed 'the *Lolita* phenomenon' is envisaged as something rather broader than just another glance at the text of this particular novel and its controversial reception. It also involves at least the noting of assorted pre-texts, a difficult publishing history, a screenplay by Nabokov, two film adaptations, and an ever-raging debate over the ever-sensitive issues of paedophilia and child abuse.

When publishing his third collection of short stories in English, in 1975, Nabokov claimed that he was 'eerily startled to meet a somewhat decrepit but unmistakable Humbert escorting his nymphet in the story I wrote almost half a century ago' (*TD* 43). In the story in question, 'A Nursery Tale' of 1926, we indeed encounter:

> a tall elderly man in evening clothes with a little girl walking beside
> – a child of fourteen or so in a low-cut black party dress....[the
> protagonist's] glance lit on the face of the child mincing at the old
> poet's side; there was something odd about that face, odd was the
> flitting glance of her much too shiny eyes, and if she were not just a
> little girl – the old man's granddaughter, no doubt – one might
> suspect that her lips were touched up with rouge. She walked
> swinging her hips very, very slightly, her legs moved close together,
> she was asking her companion something in a ringing voice... (*TD*
> 57)

Even earlier, in 1924, it is worth remembering, Nabokov had translated Lewis Carroll's *Alice in Wonderland* into Russian. In *The Gift*, a decade or so later, Boris Ivanovich Shchyogolev has his own familial situation (with step-daughter Zina Mertz) in mind when he proposes the following plot for a novel:

From real life. Imagine this kind of thing: an old dog – but still in his prime, fiery, thirsting for happiness – gets to know a widow, and she has a daughter, still quite a little girl – you know what I mean – when nothing is formed yet, but already she has a way of walking that drives you out of your mind – A slip of a girl, very fair, pale, with blue under the eyes – and of course she doesn't even look at the old goat. What to do? Well, not long thinking, he ups and marries the widow. Okay. They settle down the three of them. Here you can go on indefinitely – the temptation, the eternal torment, the itch, the mad hopes. And the upshot – a miscalculation. Time flies, he gets older, she blossoms out – and not a sausage. Just walks by and scorches you with a look of contempt. Eh? D'you feel here a kind of Dostoevskian tragedy? (G 172–3)

Here we have, almost in *mise en abyme*, two future works: *The Enchanter* and *Lolita*. The reference to Dostoevsky evokes Svidrigailov's dream in *Crime and Punishment* (involving temptation from the blandishments of a 5-year-old girl), 'Stavrogin's Confession' in *The Devils* (in which an abused girl of 12 commits suicide), and precocious sexuality in the lesser-known and uncompleted *Netochka Nezvanova*. A novel from the Russian 'Silver Age' treating somewhat similar themes is Fyodor Sologub's *The Little Demon* (1907).

What the above quotation from *The Gift* does, then, all but encompass – though without the disastrous ending tacked on – is Nabokov's novella *The Enchanter*, written in 1939 (as *Volshebnik*), and forgotten or lost for many years before its publication in Dmitri Nabokov's English translation in 1986. It is clear from a letter of 1959 that Nabokov did himself contemplate reviving this work for print (see *SL* 282–3, *E* 15–16); *The Enchanter* was scarcely, however, quite 'the first little throb of *Lolita*', as seemingly recollected in 1956 – no more than it had been totally lost or destroyed, as then thought (*E* 11–12). The unnamed enchanter's ambition toward his 12-year-old and cynically acquired step-daughter is 'to take disinterested care of her, to meld the wave of fatherhood with the wave of sexual love' (*E* 49). His voluntary death on the road, as Alfred Appel points out, is 'in a manner which Nabokov will transfer [in *Lolita*] to Charlotte Haze' (*L*, p. xxviii). It also appears to be evoked in the later novel when, in a state of insomnia at the Enchanted Hunters hotel, Humbert is aware of 'the despicable haunt of gigantic trucks roaring through the wet and windy night' (*L* 130).

'Around 1949, in Ithaca, upstate New York, the throbbing, which had never quite ceased, began to plague me again', Nabokov recalled (*E* 13). Other, perhaps minor, impulses had already restarted this throbbing a little earlier. Adam Krug, the protagonist of *Bend Sinister*, Nabokov's first novel written in America (in 1945–6), experiences the following dream about his teenage housemaid (soon revealed as a spy):

> On the night of the twelfth, he dreamt that he was surreptitiously enjoying Mariette while she sat, wincing a little, in his lap during the rehearsal of a play in which she was supposed to be his daughter. (*BS* 148)

Later, in an introduction (dated 1963) to the English version, Nabokov confirms that this amoral and treacherous young temptress had been consigned to the tender fate of gang-rape: 'the dummies are at last in quite dreadful pain, and pretty Mariette gently bleeds, staked and torn by the lust of 40 soldiers' (*BS* 8). Mallarmé's *L'Après-midi d'un Faune* is said to have haunted Krug, while *Lolita*-like vocabulary and motifs are clearly and admittedly visible (with hindsight), in sadistic association with lust and fatality (or, indeed, execution):

> Death, too, is a ruthless interruption; the widower's heavy sensuality seeks a pathetic outlet in Mariette, but as he avidly clasps the haunches of the chance nymph he is about to enjoy, a deafening din at the door breaks the throbbing rhythm forever. (*BS* 10)

Mariette, who is mortally punished, may be reminiscent of Margot (of *Laughter in the Dark*), who is not.

Notwithstanding his verdict, in a letter to Edmund Wilson of 1947, on *What Maisie Knew* as 'terrible' (*N–W* 182), and his declared antipathy to Henry James, it is difficult to believe that at least the closing stages of that novel, in which the barely teenage eponymous heroine proposes cohabitation to her stepfather Sir Claude, did not strike a chord with Nabokov, as author of *The Enchanter* and future creator of Lolita (and the word 'terrible' may even be ambiguous).[1] In any event, Nabokov certainly parodied the Jamesian style on occasions; and one may suspect that, in the case of James, as with Dostoevsky and certain others, his megaphoned distaste is at least partly attributable to a Bloomian anxiety of influence – the author in question having prematurely anticipated Nabokovian elements but without, of course, executing them quite to Nabokov's satisfaction.

Almost at the very beginning of the composition of *Lolita*, in 1948, Edmund Wilson supplied Nabokov with Volume 6 of Havelock Ellis's *Études de Psychologie Sexuelle* (Paris, 1926), which contains a hundred-page confessional document written in French by an anonymous southern Russian: 'Havelock Ellis's Russian sex masterpiece', as Wilson terms it (*N–W* 201), to which Nabokov rejoined:

> I enjoyed the Russian's love-life hugely. It is wonderfully funny. As a boy, he seems to have been quite extraordinarily lucky in coming across girls with unusually rapid and rich reactions. The end is rather bathetic. (*N–W* 202)

This apparently authentic disclosure, written down for Havelock Ellis, purports to record the detailed sexual history of the scion of an upper-crust Russian family (resident in Kiev), who develops from precociously over-sexed adolescent debauchery, involving young females of all classes, through a lengthy period of abstinence in Italy, which finally degenerates into paedophilia, voyeurism, and masturbatory obsession amid Neapolitan child prostitution. The raconteur, now known as 'Victor X', is remarkable (in Nabokovian terms) for his insistence on imagination as 'the most important factor in sexual pleasure', leading to his claim that 'I can get no enjoyment unless I can imagine the woman's enjoyment'.[2] Victor is unusually passive in his activities for much of his 'career' and restrains himself from immoral compulsion when he encounters (thanks, as in the case of Humbert, to the helping hand of a rich uncle) the stricter *mores* of Italian society – until, that is, he allows himself to be entrapped in the 'Babylon' of Naples.

While comparisons between Nabokov's protagonists and Victor should not be exaggerated, there are undeniable common factors; as Donald Rayfield (Victor's subsequent translator into English) has written, there is 'the disastrous inability to find sexual arousal and satisfaction in anything but young girls' and, moreover:

> The basic structure of *Lolita* and the confessions is similar: the contrast between the homeland (Russia or France) and the attempt to recreate lost experience in exile (Italy or America). Both Victor and Humbert Humbert are prisoners of their first childhood sexual experiences.[3]

' "Sexual confessions" (in Havelock Ellis and elsewhere), which involve tiny tots mating like mad' are mentioned in *Speak, Memory* (*SM* 158), and were elaborated slightly further in the Russian version (*Drugie berega*), which refers to 'a particularly Babylonian contribution from a landowner [from the Ukraine]'.[4]

These proto-tales and pre-texts notwithstanding, *Lolita*, of course, took on an overwhelming novelistic momentum of its own: a switch from third-person to first-person narration, a new tone in a new world – that of the post-war America which Nabokov had experienced through the 1940s and was now to recreate in fictional form at the age of 50. Nabokov later claimed to have written *Lolita* between 1949 and the spring of 1954 (*L* 312). As early as April 1947, however, he had told Wilson that he was writing 'a short novel about a man who liked little girls – and it's going to be called *The Kingdom by the Sea*' (*N–W* 188). In the early stages the heroine was to have been called 'Juanita Dark', and Nabokov was now using his index-card method of composition, adapted from lepidopteral research; field trips for the latter also provided him with a detailed topographical knowledge of many American states, while he also undertook investigations into teenage slang and relevant criminal cases. Work progressed slowly, between academic and lepidopteral exertions, but a diary entry of December 6 1953 reads: 'Finished *Lolita* which was begun exactly five years ago' (*B Am* 226).

Nabokov anticipated publishing difficulties and embarrassing repercussions from the start; accordingly, he proposed putting the novel out under an assumed name. A clue to its true authorship, however, was the inclusion of a minor character anagrammatically styled 'Vivian Darkbloom' (later to achieve further renown as the annotator of *Ada*). In the course of 1954, five prominent American publishers turned the novel down – Simon and Schuster, for one, regarding it as 'sheer pornography' (*B Am* 262). In August that year Nabokov had asked his French agent to find him a European publisher, and in February 1955 he sent the manuscript to Paris, hoping that Sylvia Beach might repeat her triumphant publication of *Ulysses*. Instead of the by now inactive Beach, however, *Lolita* attracted Maurice Girodias, proprietor of the Olympia Press. Girodias, who made his reputation in the

1950s by publishing avant-garde literary works in English of unorthodox content (including Beckett, Henry Miller, Lawrence Durrell, William Burroughs, and Jean Genet in translation) as well as unashamed pornography of a much lower class, quickly offered terms, and Nabokov accepted with alacrity. Thus began the lengthy saga of legal and financial wrangles that were to complicate the novel's eventual appearance in America. Meanwhile, Cornell sensibilities notwithstanding, Nabokov had heeded advice that pseudonymous publication might prejudice American courts against *Lolita*.

In October 1955 he received his first advance copies (having corrected galleys, but not page proofs); typographical errors there still were, but author's copyright had been withheld. A literary row in Great Britain, following Graham Greene's advocacy of *Lolita*, and a contract for a French translation with Gallimard soon raised the novel's profile, and American publishers began to bite. A package of *Lolita* excerpts with accompanying critical apparatus was devised for June 1957 publication in an occasional journal named *Anchor Review*. Copies of the Olympia Press edition, which had turned up on the black market in New York, were seized and then released by United States customs. A temporary French ban on an Olympia Press list that included *Lolita* struck a note of farce, at a time when a French-language edition was in legal preparation, along with translations for major presses in Germany and Italy. In 1958 the French ban was rescinded, Harris-Kubrick Pictures bought the film rights and, in August, with copyright problems now sorted out, *Lolita* was finally published by Putnam's in New York – only to become 'the first book since *Gone with the Wind* to sell 100,000 copies in its first three weeks' (*B Am* 365). Having soon reached number one on the bestseller list, *Lolita* was displaced – greatly to Nabokov's fury – by *Doctor Zhivago*.

Obstacles to *Lolita*'s appearance in Britain continued a little longer. The passing of the Obscene Publications Bill, however, improved the legal climate at just the right time, and Weidenfeld and Nicolson took a chance on publication of the novel in November 1959. Nigel Nicolson, himself a Conservative MP at the time, received an anonymous mid-launch-party tip-off that the book was not to be prosecuted. Although bans still came and went in a number of other countries (including France once again for a while), *Lolita* was now firmly on her way. By the mid-1980s worldwide sales had reportedly reached 14 million copies (*B Am* 387).

Lolita was, of course, greeted controversially on publication. There is no space here for a survey of its reception;[5] neither, for that matter, can anything amounting to an overall analysis of the novel be attempted. In amplification of an outline history of *Lolita* as cultural phenomenon, however, some minimal basic guidelines and suggestions for approaching the text should be delineated.

Lolita is one of the richest texts in twentieth-century literature in its use of quotation and allusion. Extratextual references and internal reverberations, long since collated in force, continue to be pinpointed and elaborated.[6] Poe, Mérimée, and Proust are usually considered the most relevant authors in this respect, with a mass of others (including Shakespeare, Goethe, de Sade, Joyce, and T. S. Eliot) close behind. Although *Lolita* appears superficially one of the least 'Russian' of Nabokov's works, a rich subtext of Russian literature also lurks.[7] Taken to task within the texture, as ever, are Nabokov's *bêtes noires*, Freud and Dostoevsky. The pickings in *Lolita* are rich for students of intertextuality and parody. Also to the fore, more unusually, are the consumerism and popular culture of post-war America between 1947 and 1952; Fredric Jameson singles out Nabokov, 'a foreigner to begin with', for his timely handling of such material in *Lolita*, 'which thereby at once became The Great American Novel'; for Angela Carter, *Lolita* was 'the Camp masterpiece of its decade'.[8]

Clichéd as it may be to stress this, *Lolita* the novel – no easy soft-porn read to begin with – is heavily dependent on (and expressly designed for) re-reading for any real level of textual comprehension. And even this only serves to highlight a plethora of narratalogical problems. *Lolita* is ostensibly a first-person confessional narrative, composed in jail on the verge of a fatal heart attack by Humbert Humbert (a cultured European immigrant, French scholar, and would-be *littérateur*): the quirky chronicle of his deviant obsession with pre- and early teenage 'nymphets'; his domination – and subsequent loss – of a cynically acquired stepdaughter, Dolores Haze ('Lolita', aged

12 to 14); and the murder in revenge of her supposed abductor, an American playwright named Clare Quilty.

Humbert's narrative is prefaced by a 'Foreword' from one 'John Ray, Jr., Ph.D.', editor of the manuscript. This Gothic device of the posthumous manuscript from jail is as problematic here in its effects as with its predecessors in sensational fiction. The extent of Ray's 'editing' cannot be known; Humbert's 'bizarre cognomen' is his [the manuscript's author's] own invention (*L* 3); all names, except the heroine's first name, are disguised. There is at least one chronological disparity (to which we shall return below). Although Humbert's criminality is established by Ray's Foreword, the first-time reader is unsure of the indictment until the end of the narrative; or, to put it another way, the novel is not a 'who dunnit?', but a 'what dun he?', with the name of the victim, rather than the killer, withheld. In addition, Humbert acknowledges bouts of institutionalized insanity. What weight does the reader attach to this insanity, and its recurrence, in endeavouring to measure the sincerity of a self-declared trickster and liar? Anyone familiar with Nabokov's *œuvre*, or with the techniques of Nikolai Gogol, should at least suspect the presence (or rather the absence!) of a story behind the story. How much of the 'real' story do we get, and what can we trust of what we do get?

We have already stressed that *Lolita* purports to be Humbert's confession. It can equally therefore be seen as (fictional – but at what level?) autobiography or memoir. It also poses, at least, as a psychological case-study (both medical and criminological) and a legal disposition. It goes without saying that *Lolita* is generally read as a novel, although the apportioning to it of a romantic as against a realist emphasis is entirely another matter. It may be seen to play upon the picaresque or the crime novel; it may be imbued with romance, faery, or even lepidoptery. Mythic readings are also on the agenda; according to Lance Olsen, for instance, *Lolita* 'reworks and perverts the Pygmalion myth'.[9] Its prime impetus may come from the decadence of Nabokov's native Russian Symbolism, or equally from the Western tradition of Huysmans, Wilde, and the prominently featured 'Aubrey' (in the text as 'McFate' and as the town of 'Beardsley').

In an essay first published in 1989, Trevor McNeely divides critical argument on *Lolita* into two categories: that based on aesthetics and that based on character. The first, according to which Nabokov has constructed a devilishly cunning game, renders the novel (or so the argument goes) ultimately pointless. Those wishing to promote *Lolita* as a great literary work on the basis of Humbert's moral (character) development, for that matter, face an uphill struggle in avoiding implicit support for paedophile rights. The way out of this bind, taken by all too many a commentator in McNeely's view, is an unprincipled and selective blending of the two approaches. The calculated hoax perpetrated on a gullible literary and academic establishment and the resultant status still enjoyed by *Lolita* therefore represent 'Nabokov's triumph as a trickster'.[10] McNeely's resolution of what he calls 'the *Lolita* riddle' may overstate its case, but it nevertheless raises interesting points.

There can be little doubt that a 'straight reading' of *Lolita* (as a 'realistic' confessional novel, taken at face value) leads to severe narratological as well as ethical difficulties: whose face? and what value? Martin Amis calls it 'both irresistible and unforgivable'.[11] Richard H. Bullock, in an article first published in 1984, clarifies a problem that has beset much *Lolita* criticism: the lack of discrimination by many commentators between Humbert as character and Humbert as narrator.[12] This has led to much pointless speculation as to what Humbert (as character) understands within the narrative of Humbert (as narrator, recorder after the event or, indeed, novelist). Such confusion, no doubt, also chimes with the 'having it both ways' analyses complained of by McNeely. Contradictory statements by Humbert, his own remarks on time, his admitted mental disturbance, an assortment of incoherencies and dubieties in verisimilitude (which cannot be listed in detail here, but surface in many a critical discussion of the novel) all combine to render any verification of authenticity an impossibility (as, indeed, is the case in many a first-person narrative lacking in corroborative evidence). How, given all of this, can we test Humbert's claim that it was Lolita who seduced him, or that she was already no virgin, let alone the veracity or significance of his childhood (pre)history with Annabel Leigh or, for that matter, his ultimate 'moral apotheosis' (Ray's 'Foreword', *L* 5)?

The apparent chronological discrepancy, involving the number of days in which Humbert purportedly wrote his text, as against the number of calendar days that could have passed according to his narrative, leads some critics to suspect that the action proper in *Lolita* ceases on 22 September 1952, the day Humbert is supposed to have received a letter from Lolita (now Dolly, or Mrs Richard, Schiller).[13] The immediate consequence of such an interpretation is to remove the visit to Dolly Schiller, and indeed the subsequent murder of Quilty, into the realms of fantasy. Humbert might therefore have been jailed 'merely' for some offence connected with child molestation. The role and 'reality' of Quilty become even more speculative. Such a reading has recently won powerful critical backing.[14]

However, it could be that there is no need to stop there when working backwards to isolate a shift-point into fantasy. Ray himself, whose prose style is not merely Nabokovian but approximates to Humbertian *skaz*, may be an invention of the 'real' narrator masked by the name Humbert Humbert.[15] In this case the entire novel would be the work of 'Humbert', who may not after all be in jail and may not (in 1955, as claimed) even be dead. The story behind the story may resemble *Lolita*, to a greater or lesser degree, or the chronicle may be a work of pure fantasy. In any event, as Dolinin argues, '[w]hat is criminal is not the protagonist's erotic reverie as such..., but his desire to impose it on the outside world'; on the other hand, his 'real' past may be 'too ugly, mean and meaningless for [Humbert's project of] "Proustianization"'.[16]

So, what would this leave us with? A poetic rhapsody of despair in the decadent tradition, all Humbert Humbert's, whoever he may really be and whatever may have happened in 'reality' (for which there has been no shortage of suggestions). Humbert apart, 'Lolita' – or Dolly Haze – may or may not have existed. Chronological difficulties have gone, as have those concerning the 'realism' of Quilty and many other problematic details. The reliance on contrivance, at one level at least, is avoided, as are disputes over the verisimilitude and sincerity of Humbert's 'performance'; the problem of his reliability recedes. A narratological hierarchy is thereby established, reaching from Humbert as character to Humbert as narrator, or even as author (who cannot be denied aesthetic credit for his artistic pretension *and* achievement, regardless of his ethical duplicity); at a close remove is the implied author of *Lolita*,[17] who is capable of such metafictional twists as the introduction of one 'Vivian

Darkbloom' and nods towards other Nabokov texts (such as *The Enchanter*: textual features that surely *are* beyond our Humbert). The reader, by the end of the novel, is forthwith catapulted back via John Ray to Humbert – as both character and narrator – in a circular process that mutates, with the benefit of initial read(s), into a (re)cognitive spiral.

This brings us directly to Nabokov's Russian version of *Lolita* – the only one of his English novels that he 'Russianed', a process which he himself likened to 'starting a new spiral' (*SO* 52). He regarded the result, to an extent at least, as disappointing.[18] Nabokov began what he found to be the difficult task of reverse translation in 1963, to avoid the day when, otherwise, 'some oaf within or without Russia will translate and publish the book' (*B Am* 472); ironically, what he most feared very nearly came to pass, despite his efforts, when the novel was first considered for publication in the late Soviet period of *glasnost'*.[19] Nabokov's Russian *Lolita*, indeed, following its publication in 1967, met with a mixed reception among such Russians as managed then to read it. The subject matter, the use of anglicisms, and the reversion to a Russian prose style unfamiliar since the days of the Silver Age, the modernist prose of the 1920s and, not least, the works of Sirin, caused paroxysms in some. However, a number of influential Russian *literati*, then as now, such as Nina Berberova (a leading member of Nabokov's own émigré generation) and commentators currently at the cutting edge of Anglo-Russian Nabokov studies hold his last Russian text in the highest esteem as a contribution to the evolution of Russian prose.[20]

What is more, in the view of Dolinin at least, a close study of the Russian version, which he considers 'a *new redaction* of the novel' [Dolinin's emphasis], if anything confirms the plausibility of the type of reading outlined above. Nabokov made some literary references explicit and inserted certain chronological minutiae (without, though, correcting the important 'discrepancy' on which such a reading largely depends). However, he may also, as Dolinin believes, have been exploiting 'self-translation as a powerful tool for self-exegesis' (*GCVN* 324). More problematic, perhaps, is the tendency to russify some literary allusions and, apparently, endow Humbert's consciousness with a more overt Russian cultural layer absent from the original. If one accepts the view that Nabokov's ideal bilingual reader would absorb and merge the two texts, then this can only strengthen the metafictional interpretation of interference and control within the fictional world by the implied author(s), at a chronological distance of a decade and more. Vivian Darkbloom transmogrifies into (the more Russian Symbolist but equally anagrammatic) 'Vivian Damor-Blok', and so the spiral swirls on. However, the vast majority of Nabokov's readers will remain confined to either the English or the Russian *Lolita*.

Improbably yet predictably, there was a Broadway musical of *Lolita* that duly flopped in 1971 (by Alan Jay Lerner and John Barry) and a later, equally unsuccessful, stage version (by Edward Albee: flopped 1981, published 1984). Adaptations have, however, played a colossal role in keeping *Lolita* in the public consciousness through the two film versions.

In the summer of 1958 Harris-Kubrick Pictures enquired about the film rights to *Lolita* and within weeks a deal had been done. The following summer Nabokov was invited to Hollywood to write the screenplay himself. A tentative visit to the film capital did not yield positive ideas, but an autumnal stay in Sicily did, and financial terms were agreed, with an extra payment to be added if Nabokov received sole credit for the screenplay (which, indeed, he did). Six months were spent writing it, off Sunset Boulevard, in 1960, though rights to publish it were denied. After a certain amount of argument and a lot of cutting, James Harris and Stanley Kubrick declared it 'the best screenplay ever written in Hollywood' (*B Am* 408): not that this prevented them from drastically reworking it and then adding extemporizations. The film opened in New York on 13 June 1962, in Nabokov's presence; he praised the acting, but summed up the end product privately as 'a lovely misty view seen through mosquito netting' (*B Am* 466). The film was a modest box-office success.

Kubrick's *Lolita* is indeed shot in a misty black and white and was, in the event, filmed in England – partly for financial reasons and partly due to Peter Sellers' commitments and his divorce case.[21] Sue Lyon is older than Lolita (15 at the time of shooting, though still a little young for her final scene), yet her kittenish performance remains striking. James Mason manages with considerable aplomb a suave, pedantic, and obsequious European pose as Humbert (a role that Olivier had momentarily accepted). Shelley Winters makes the most of Charlotte. However, for most filmgoers, the show was stolen by Peter Sellers' bravura improvizations in the expanded role of Quilty. Much, of course, is telescoped or omitted (there is, for instance, no Annabel, Valechka, or Rita, and no Lolita playing tennis). The setting has been moved forward a decade to the late 1950s (obvious from the cars and the Nelson Riddle score and, were there to be any doubt, confirmed by the crack about Doctors Schweitzer and Zhivago); indeed, the subsequent published version of the screenplay was to tell us, upon Humbert's arrival at the Haze home, 'It is now 1960' (*LS* 733). Any cinematic adaptation of a novel is forced to make interpretive choices and usually a straight realist reading will be suggested. Mistiness apart, the 'reality' of the plot is not in question.[22] The shooting of Quilty, in a remarkable opening sequence that in itself justifies Pauline Kael's view of the film as 'black slapstick',[23] frames the narrative, with vestiges of Humbert's narration being retained; instead of the 'what dun he?' of the book, the film gives us a 'why did he?' As a movie, Kubrick's production retains its interest, as its not infrequent television showings prove.

Commentators frequently wish that Kubrick had waited a few years to make *Lolita*, by which time the censorship restrictions would have eased. As it was, the 1961 shooting was closely attended by British censor John Trevelyan. The casting of an older Lolita, however, and the restriction of sexuality largely to whisper and innuendo, resulted in little enough trouble. The overall effect, in Richard Corliss's view, was to transform Humbert's fixation into 'an obsession but not a perversion' and Kubrick's *Lolita* into 'the story of an abused stepfather'. Adrian Lyne's 1990s remake was to be rather a different matter.

Meanwhile, by 1972 Nabokov had finally extracted permission from Kubrick to publish his original screenplay (except that it wasn't quite either of the originals), and this finally appeared in 1974. The screenplay, bearing Nabokov's name, as used in the Kubrick film, has never appeared in published form. Nabokov's original mammoth version languishes in the Nabokov archive, and we are dependent on Boyd for a description of it (see *B Am* 408–14 on the screenplays). The only published *Lolita* screenplay is a further version of the shortened one that Nabokov had delivered to Kubrick and Harris (now labelled 'Summer 1960 Los Angeles' and 'revised December 1973 Montreux': *LS* 833). Reduced though it may have been, it is still far too long for a film of normal length (*LS* 677–833 on the printed page, Nabokov's directions included; while Kubrick's film, at 152 minutes, is not exactly short). *Lolita: A Screenplay* includes many scenes dropped by Kubrick and not in the original novel. Dr John Ray appears as a sub-narrating character; a confusing number of extra minor characters are introduced; and additional Humbert–Quilty encounters cause a diminution of the latter's 'spectral shimmer' (*B Am* 413). The first version, in Boyd's estimation, 'is diffuse and often strangely pedestrian' (*B Am* 409). In 1973 Nabokov saw the published one as 'a vivacious variant of an old novel' (*LS* 676). Richard Corliss has called Kubrick's *Lolita* 'a vivacious variant on a treacherous theme'.[24] Any film adaptation is, by definition, not the novel; neither, for that matter, can any screenplay version – even one by Nabokov himself – persuasively sway perceptions of the novel. *Lolita: A Screenplay* cannot have the textual status of the Russian *Lolita*, even if the latter can be admitted into textual complementarity. Nevertheless, one might hope some day for, say, a serialized television production of one of Nabokov's screenplays.

In 1990 the Carolco independent film company secured the remake rights to *Lolita* for $1 million. Adrian Lyne was to direct and, financial problems apart, again there were complications over a screenplay (involving submissions by Harold Pinter, David Mamet, and James Dearden), before the task fell to Stephen Schiff. Following the conclusion of shooting in 1996, the film encountered serious distribution problems, due to the climate of acute anxiety over child abuse developing through the western world from the 1980s. The timing of its completion coincided with fresh anti-child-pornography legislation in the United States and a series of current or recent sensational cases (by no means analogous – it goes without saying – to *Lolita*, ranging from Roman Polanski, to Amy Fisher, to JonBenét Ramsey) in that country, as well as those in Great Britain and in Belgium. Denied a distributor in a number of countries, including the United States (where it was finally acquired by the Showtime cable channel), Lyne's *Lolita* began to be shown in Europe in September 1997 and opened in London in May 1998.

Advance calls for a ban in Britain soon faded, giving way to a view that the film is too long and boring to provide unseemly encouragement to actual or potential paedophiles.

Of a comparable length to Kubrick's *Lolita* (in fact sixteen minutes shorter), Lyne's film, for all its not inconsiderable visual accomplishment, lacks the style, the wit, and in particular the tone achieved by Kubrick. This is due perhaps as much to the casting as to the direction: Jeremy Irons is far too English for the cosmopolitan European-accented Humbert, while Quilty (played by Frank Langella) is reduced to a sinister presence in the shadows, shorn of any charisma and most of his repartee. The schematic quality of the repellent execution scene, in which Humbert exorcises his dark self, and his emergence as a shivering but righteous wreck, serve to exacerbate the ethical blurring current in a society in which, as one reviewer has put it, 'we sexualize the representation of children while demonizing those who respond sexually to them'.[25] Lyne's film, by and large, sticks closer to the novel than Kubrick's: he does set the action where it belongs, back in the late 1940s, and he inserts a range of short scenes omitted by his predecessor. However, the 'road movie' accentuation results in the omission or reduction of a number of Kubrick's more successful elements. The most notable inclusion is the Annabel Leigh prologue, but this is less than literally faithful to its original in the novel, and Lyne unaccountably misses the opportunity to double Annabel with the actress playing Lolita (herself gamely enough essayed by Dominique Swain).

The name 'Lolita', as well as the word 'nymphet', has entered the language, and both have acquired worldwide connotations while simultaneously achieving a dubious commercial (and in particular, of late, an Internet) sexploitation. In 1959 Nabokov began a poem, which parodied Pasternak's 'The Nobel Prize', with the verse:

> What is the evil deed I have committed?
> Seducer, criminal – is this the word
> for me who set the entire world a-dreaming
>   of my poor little girl?

> (*PP* 147)

He might well at that time not have suspected that the same question would still be needing to be asked on his behalf forty years on.

'Pale Fire'/*Pale Fire*

> ...I'll example you with thievery:
> The sun's a thief, and with his great attraction
> Robs the vast sea; the moon's an arrant thief,
> And her pale fire she snatches from the sun;
> The sea's a thief...
>
> *(Timon of Athens*, IV. iii)

Nabokov, as we have seen, complained that Henry James had not demonstrated the poetical prowess of his imaginary poet, Jeffrey Aspern, in *The Aspern Papers* (N–W 53). To take another instance, however, Boris Pasternak's attempt to do that very thing on behalf of Iurii Zhivago was evidently not of itself sufficient to allow him to escape Nabokov's sharp censure. In the case of his own fiction, Nabokov had earlier given plentiful examples of the works (poetical and prose) of Fyodor in *The Gift*; when he came to write *Pale Fire*, he was to create the eponymous 999-line, 4-canto narrative poem ascribed to his protagonist, the imaginary American poet John Francis Shade (1898–1959). Not that Shade is necessarily to be considered the principal protagonist of the novel that bears the name of his supposed poetic creation; that honour, in the view of many commentators (although the matter remains debatable, as does just about everything else in *Pale Fire*), would belong to the figure best known as Charles Kinbote, Shade's posthumous editor. Nothing in a novel by Nabokov, though, is ever going to be as simple as all that.

Nabokov later nominated Shade's 'American poem' as 'the hardest stuff I ever had to compose' (*SO* 55); as for Shade's own bardic rating, Nabokov declared him 'by far the greatest of *invented* poets' (*SO* 59). Brian Boyd accords 'Pale Fire' – the poem – 'all the assurance of a masterpiece', going so far as to consider that 'English poetry has few things better to offer than "Pale

Fire"' (*B Am* 439–40). Others are rather more underwhelmed: it has been called 'a bumbling poem by bumbling John Shade', 'a seriously flawed masterpiece', and 'good only in spots'.[1] Marianna Torgovnick, author of the last remark, may well be justified in her view that any attempt at evaluation of Shade's poem itself involves succumbing to one of Nabokov's many traps. Shade appears to consider himself 'just behind / (one oozy footstep) [Robert] Frost' ('PF' ll. 425–6). 'Pale Fire' is not without its powerful passages, but neither is it without its (quite possibly fully intended) infelicities. In any event, it was written, and situated within *Pale Fire*, for particular purposes: both to be glossed and itself to gloss the gloss, as the principal embedded text in a complex interactive (or perhaps interchangeable) process between author/writer–narrator–character–reader.

Pale Fire the novel, then, purports to be a glorified – and is indeed an eccentric – edition of the late John Shade's final poem, 'Pale Fire' (1959), under the tender redaction of this certain Charles Kinbote. The text consists of a 'Foreword'; 'Pale Fire: A Poem in Four Cantos'; a lengthy 'Commentary' (taking up about three-quarters of the whole); and an 'Index'. If 'Foreword' and 'Index' would traditionally be considered as belonging to the 'paratext',[2] they are here clearly to be seen as components of a highly singular novelistic structure. Even the epigraph (an oddball passage from Boswell's *Life of Samuel Johnson*), situated after the dedication ('to Véra') and before the 'Contents' page (listing the four components as just mentioned), similarly belongs to the text proper (we may assume, given a reference to this source in the Commentary: *PF* 125). This leaves as genuine paratext the title-page and cover, ascribing *Pale Fire* to Vladimir Nabokov, together with certain 'epitexts', or authorial statements from beyond the text (whatever value we may wish to accord these). Such a structure clearly evokes Nabokov's mammoth edition of *Eugene Onegin* (itself by no means devoid of eccentricities, and effectively completed as *Pale Fire* was envisaged), as more than one commentator has pointed out, and the creation of a parody of such an editorial-critical process is undoubtedly one the exercises carried through by its author in *Pale Fire*.

John Shade's poem seems to be largely autobiographical in

content, focusing in particular on the suicide by drowning of his daughter Hazel (Canto 2), and including agnostic musings on the vague possibility, at least, of an afterlife.[3] Charles Kinbote, who styles himself a refugee from the recently revolutionized state of Zembla (purportedly a northern neighbour of Russia) and a recently appointed professor (of Zemblan studies?) at the University of Wordsmith (at New Wye, Appalachia), has taken up residence as a neighbour of the Shades. Much taken with Shade's poetry, which he 'had tried to put into Zemblan two decades earlier!' (*PF* 18), Kinbote, who also claims really (and secretly) to be the exiled king of Zembla (lecturing *incognito* at an American liberal arts college) imposes himself on Shade's society (to the annoyance of Shade's wife, Sybil), with the purpose of inspiring in Shade an epic poem on the Zemblan land and its recent history. This is the poem that Kinbote takes Shade to have written, only slightly daunted by its apparent lack of correspondence to any such theme or content. This 'rent-a-poet' obsession impels Kinbote to appropriate Shade's poem (composed, in true Nabokovian fashion, on a bundle of index cards) as the poet meets an untimely end: mistakenly shot, Kinbote affirms, by a would-be regicide named Jacob Gradus. The poem is then (mis)read, (re)interpreted, and stretched to breaking-point in Kinbote's Commentary to fit his thesis that it had really been intended as a *poème à clef* on Zembla and its exiled king. The wacky index reinforces this act of literary theft and critical superimposition – or, as Genette puts it, 'textual appropriation … supported by the unlimited submission of any text to any hermeneutic, however unscrupulous the latter may be'.[4]

Such, at least, is the surface story. As for the 'real, real story, the story underneath' (*PF*, p. vii), this has been a matter for endless debate. Since Mary McCarthy's seminal review article of 1962 (in its latest incarnation it appears as the 'Introductory Essay' to the Penguin edition: *PF*, pp. v–xxii), it has been widely held that 'Kinbote', regardless of his claims to be '*Charles II*, Charles Xavier Vseslav, last king of Zembla, surnamed The Beloved' (*PF* 240: 'surname' here being used by Kinbote in its less common sense of 'sobriquet'), is in 'reality' one '*Botkin, V.*, American scholar of Russian descent' (*PF* 240) – thus styled in the Index and mentioned in passing in the text of the Commentary (*PF* 125 and 210; and alluded to, 175). Similarly,

'Gradus' is almost certainly Jack Grey, an escaped psychopath, who, rather than missing his aim at the 'king', mistakes Shade for Judge Goldsworth (the owner of the house rented by Kinbote, whom John Shade happens to resemble). Grey (with or without his many pseudonyms) is therefore in all probability not the foreign Shadow hit-man Kinbote makes him out to be, but merely one of 'the terrifying shadows that Judge Goldsworth's gown threw across the underworld' (PF 71): a natural-born revenge killer who gets the wrong man.

Kinbote-Botkin (or, for simplicity's sake, at least, we may continue to refer to him as 'Kinbote'),[5] contrary to his declared intentions, has indeed constructed from his 'unambiguous *apparatus criticus*' 'the monstrous semblance of a novel' (PF 71). His Commentary constitutes, in the main, a fantasy narrative approaching novelistic proportions, pegged onto and around the initial Shade poem. Just as Hermann Karlovich of *Despair* mistakes his supposed double, Kinbote (perhaps wilfully, certainly perversely) mistakes Shade's 'Pale Fire', blaming its apparent lack of true resemblance to its Kinbotean-Platonic ideal on the wiles aforethought of the hostile Sybil. All the eventual interpenetrations of theme and imagery throughout the component levels of *Pale Fire* would thus appear to be attributable ultimately and solely to the editorial machinations of Kinbote and his fixation on producing a 'rival other text'.[6]

Arguments over whether a primary author for the entire text (other than at the level of Nabokov himself, of course) can be discerned (could Shade have 'faked' his own demise and imagined the mad Kinbote? could Kinbote have written Shade's poem as well?) by now seem largely beside the point. Nevertheless, it is worth saying that the 'Occam's razor' interpretation – that Shade wrote 'Pale Fire' and that Kinbote produced the rest – retains majority support; in any event, the notion that Shade might himself have authored Kinbote's contributions has been effectively demolished by D. Barton Johnson's comment that Shade lacks the necessary Russian background and knowledge also to 'be' Kinbote.[7] Or, to put it another way, as Marianna Torgovnick has observed, Kinbote (plus Charles II, plus no doubt Botkin, and certainly Nabokov) all have the quality of exile about them; Shade (as a thorough-going American academic poet, steeped in English verse) does not. Such discussions, which raged on and off for thirty years or more, are now to be seen as a distraction from the narrative technicalities and intertextual puzzles that genuinely dominate *Pale Fire*.

In the terminology of Russian Formalist criticism, the *siuzhet* of *Pale Fire* (the plot-content of the novel as presented to the reader) may be indicated as above. The *fabula* (the 'fable', or what 'really' happened) is, as we have already seen, another matter; as with some of Gogol's stories, the fable is buried well below the surface story (such as that may be) and is problematic, to say the least, to pinpoint. The possibilities are several, if not unlimited. Beyond the questions of authorship raised above, the following scenarios can be offered.

1. Kinbote *is* Charles Xavier and Zembla is 'real' (within the fictional world of the novel): in which case, perhaps, Kinbote is *not* so mad after all.

2. Kinbote thinks he is Charles Xavier and there is, or is not, a real Zembla: in either case, it may be assumed, Kinbote *is* mad.

3. Kinbote is really Botkin and the circumstances of number 2 above apply (this seems to have been the scenario favoured by Nabokov himself!).

4. Kinbote, who is, or is not, really Botkin, consciously invents Charles Xavier and Zembla, but is also obsessed with Shade and his poetic talent.

5. As in number 4 above, but with Kinbote consciously usurping the identity of (a real) Charles Xavier of Zembla (with whom, as with Shade, he is obsessed).

In many, if not all, of these scenarios (which certainly do not exhaust all possibilities), Kinbote has to be accorded considerable artistic talent, alongside his obsessive editorial opportunism and exploitation. Pekka Tammi, perhaps the most rigorous commentator on Nabokov's schemes of narration, declares that '*while Shade remains in control of the artistic system of the poem, it is Kinbote who is responsible for the system of the comprehensive narrative text as a work of art*' [emphasis in the original].[8] In any event, the mode of reading of *Pale Fire* as an entity demands, or at least elicits, instruction from Kinbote himself (see *PF* 25: the notes are to take precedence and are to be read three times) and has itself inspired expert commentary.[9]

Another issue that has aroused rather pointless argument is the question of the 'reality' or otherwise of Zembla. Real or fairy-tale, as the case may be, within the fictional universe of *Pale Fire*, 'Zembla is Semblance', as Mary McCarthy put it (*PF*, p. ix). It has been observed to be an *Alice in Wonderland* sphere, a setting of Ruritanian romance, deriving conceivably in part from Anthony Hope's *The Prisoner of Zenda* (1894) and certainly from a variety of other sources, and spliced with carnivalistic inversions. Charles Xavier, its last monarch, is a rampantly gay composite of Charles II of England, Bonnie Prince Charlie, and perhaps the neo-Romantic fantasist king of Bavaria, Ludwig II. Gogol's protagonist Poprishchin, of *The Diary of a Madman*, who suddenly decides he is the king of Spain, also deserves mention.[10] For all its supposed northernness, the Zemblan revolution and seizure of power by the Extremists, unlikely as this may at first seem, may owe something to the nearest revolution to it temporally – that of Castro in Cuba (in 1958–9). Onhava, 'the beautiful capital of Zembla' (*PF* 245), for all its supposed Zemblan-Eskimo derivation, is a near-anagram of Havana. Moreover, which current event would play on the mind of an anti-Soviet Russian émigré (such as Nabokov, or his *alter ego* Botkin) if not Castro's revolution, bringing the prospect of Soviet interference into America's backyard?[11] In any event, Nabokov himself, it should perhaps be noted, was no monarchist.[12]

In other respects, Zembla remains firmly northern (mythologically, culturally, and linguistically), although its supposed exile (Charles Xavier/Kinbote) seems remarkably disconcerted by a harsh New England winter (*PF* 18). Priscilla Meyer, in her fascinating monograph on *Pale Fire*, has established that one intertextual layer of the novel amounts to an outline cultural history of the North spanning a thousand years, and has identified a sweeping range of allusions to swathes of northern source material: Russian, Scandinavian, Anglo-Saxon, English (and – or rather – of the British Isles), and Germanic.[13] Input from other cultures, such as those of North America and France, has to be accommodated, as do certain special Nabokovian preoccupations. These are both biographical (the mistaken assassination of the father) and textually self-referential (in particular, narrative threads from the abandoned Russian novel *Solus Rex* and the fancies of Victor Wind from *Pnin*).

Without rehearsing this in detail here, a brief reminder of the main referential building blocks, along with one or two suggested additions (the possibilities for which seem almost endless), may go some modest way towards delineating Nabokov's intertextual design. Novaya Zemlya and Severnaya Zemlya (meaning 'New' and 'Northern Land' respectively) are substantial Arctic islands to the north of Russia. As such, presumably, they gave rise to the mentions of (Nova) Zembla in works by Pope and Swift (*Essay on Man, Dunciad, The Battle of the Books* – frequently noted in Nabokov scholarship) and here undergo transformation into a lost Arcadia. Another evocation of 'Nova Zembla' that could not have failed to appeal to a Kinbote–Botkin–Nabokov (or, for that matter, to Shade, the eighteenth-century specialist) is contained in a paragraph of *Tristram Shandy*, in 'The Author's Preface' within Volume III:

Indeed there is one thing to be considered, that in Nova Zembla, North Lapland, and in all those cold and dreary tracts of the globe, which lie more directly under the arctic and antarctic circles, – where the whole province of man's concernments lies for near nine months together, within the narrow compass of his cave, – where the spirits are compressed almost to nothing, – and where the passions of a man, with every thing that belongs to them, are as frigid as the zone itself; – there the least quantity of *judgment* imaginable does the business, – and of *wit*, – there is a total and an absolute saving, – for as not one spark is wanted, – so not one spark is given. Angels and ministers of grace defend us! What a dismal thing it would have been to have governed a kingdom, to have fought a battle, or made a treaty, or run a match, or wrote a book, or got a child, or held a provincial chapter there, with so *plentiful a lack* of wit and judgment about us! for mercy's sake! let us think no more about it, but travel on as fast as we can southwards into Norway, – crossing over Swedeland, if you please, through the small triangular province of Angermania to the lake of Bothnia; coasting along it through east and west Bothnia, down to Carelia, and so on, through all those states and provinces which border upon the far side of the Gulf of Finland, and the north-east of the Baltic, up to Petersbourg, and just stepping into Ingria; – then stretching over directly from thence through the north parts of the Russian empire – leaving Siberia a little upon the left hand till we get into the very heart of Russian and Asiatic Tartary.[14]

John Shade's poetic mentors are Pope and Wordsworth; Hazel Shade's name may be taken from Scott's *The Lady of the Lake* (McCarthy, *PF*, p. xv), though, once again, it is also to be located in a number of other sources.[15] Browning and Yeats are among a range of further poetic contributors. Norse and Anglo-Saxon sources have been attributed, as have more modern works from German Romanticism (Goethe's *Erlkönig* and Bürger's *Lenore*) and Scandinavian fairy or Gothic tale (Hans Andersen and Isak Dinesen – the latter, of course, Karen Blixen, a Dane writing in English).[16]

Shakespeare's *Timon of Athens* (IV. iii) is the ostensible source of the dual title (of poem and novel), as Kinbote indirectly reveals even through his bumbling Zemblan mis(re-)translation. However, for all the resonances of thievery and solar-lunar imagery pervading *Pale Fire*, Meyer may well be justified in pointing to Shakespeare's other usage of 'pale fire', in *Hamlet*, as at least equally central:

> The glowworm shows the matin to be near
> And 'gins to pale his ineffectual fire.
> Adieu, adieu, adieu. Remember me.

(I. v. 96–8)

These words of King Hamlet's ghost represent the revenge theme for parental murder or loss that she sees as crucial to much of Nabokov's work (not least the shooting of Shade in *Pale Fire*).[17]

Kinbote is pursued by the 'Shadeans': academic followers of John Shade who dispute Kinbote's right and suitability to produce the posthumous edition of their idol's last poem. King Charles Xavier is pursued by the 'Shadows', a fanatical regicide wing of the Zemblan Extremist party (personified by Jacob Gradus, 'alias Jack Degree, de Grey, d'Argus . . . etc.': *PF* 241). Shade, seen as 'deeply involved with death',[18] whose name is in any case an anagram of Hades, is slain not by a Shadean but by a Shadow, the grey man Gradus (who is probably really Jack Grey). Kinbote, whose kingly escape had been aided by identically scarlet-clad decoys, each posing as a 'counterfeit king' (*PF* 116), expects to be besieged by further Shadows ('a bigger, more respectable, more competent Gradus': *PF* 236). Shakespeare's King Richard III was assailed by shadows before Bosworth and by multiple would-be kings ('six Richmonds in the field': V. vii. 11) in the battle; counterfeit kings in battle also feature in *Henry IV, Part 1* (V. iv). The shadow Shakespeare casts over *Pale Fire* is certainly a long one.

A remarkable 'shadow tale' (in addition to Andersen's *The Shadow*) from German Romanticism also warranting mention is *Peter Schlemihl, the Shadowless Man* by Chamisso, an exile from the French Revolution, writing in German, who was also a naturalist and a poet. One can plausibly assume Nabokov to have known this work, which he is likely to have read perhaps in an English translation (possibly even in the Cassell's National Library edition quoted here).[19] Peter Schlemihl has acquired unlimited wealth by trading his shadow to a man in grey for a magic purse. Repenting of his bargain (or doubting *gold's worth*), in the face of the all-but-total ostracism he unexpectedly encounters as a shadowless man, he initially finds that 'the grey man has disappeared like a shadow'. Posing as 'Count Peter', he is taken by some for the king of Prussia, or for 'some proscribed prince or illustrious exile':

> It appeared soon after, from accounts in the newspapers, that the whole history of the King of Prussia's fictitious journey originated in mere idle report. But a king I was, and a king I must remain by all means; and one of the richest and most royal, although people were at a loss to know where my territories lay. (*Peter Schlemihl*, 50)

Unable, due to his deficiency (the only remedy for which would be 'to exchange my soul for my shadow'), 'to remain in a country where I seemed to be *beloved*' (my emphasis), he finally rids himself of his grey tormentor by hurling the bottomless purse into an abyss, and embarks on a life of wandering from polar region to polar region, with the aid of seven-league boots, and natural study.

Before this, Schlemihl had been faithfully served by 'the *Argus*-eyed Bendel' (my emphasis) but was robbed and betrayed by another servant, the 'prodigious thief' named Rascal. In one sequence, he gives hot pursuit to a loose 'shadow of a man not unlike my own', and later receives a temporary loan of his own shadow (the grey man assuring him that 'the devil is not so black as he is painted'). Kinbote's parenthesized remark in the Foreword 'as our shadows still walk without us' (*PF* 14) may owe something to Chamisso, while Schlemihl's allusion to discussion with his tempter of 'the question of questions – the answer that should solve all mysteries' suggests the 'Ultima Thule' theme in Nabokov and Shade's metaphysical questing. The relationship between shadow and soul, the reverberations of loss, and the solar-lunar implications of shadow and thievery resonate through *Pale Fire*, from Timon's Athens to Charles Xavier's Zembla.

The interpenetrations and the merging of levels in *Pale Fire*, which have disconcerted many readers,[20] are based, among other things, on mirrors and reflections, patterns and coincidences, and intertextual correspondences. Sudarg of Bokay, mirror-maker *extraordinaire* of Zembla and 'patron saint' (*PF* 247), is a palindromic (re)version of Jakob Gradus (d'Argus). Shades and shadows have been extensively noted already. 'I was the shadow of the waxwing slain' is the first line (and is also line 131; and – if we wish to believe Kinbote – would have been added as line 1000) of 'Pale Fire'. The waxwing, at least in England, where Judge Goldsworth had gone, is a visitor from Scandinavia. In the melodramatic finale in the Goldsworth garden, as Douglas Fowler puts it, 'Shade dead, Kinbote clutches the shade of Shade, the (literally) immortal poem'.[21] And so the waxwing flies on.

The incoherent message received by Hazel Shade at the spiritualist session in the barn ('pada ata lane pad not ogo old wart alan ther tale feur far rant lant tal told', *PF* 151), supposed, or partially decoded by many, as a vague warning of her father's future murder three years later – for which purpose (as 'Pa data'!) it proves, not surprisingly, useless – is more plausibly a red herring, deflecting attention from a self-prefiguration of her own suicide encoded in Shade's poem.[22] Vladimir Alexandrov has pointed out that Kinbote himself apparently fails to notice a number of parallels between 'Pale Fire' and his own story.[23] These are constantly being added to, so another offering here might not be out of place. When Kinbote visits Shade, who is shaving in his bath (*PF* 207–8), the latter recounts how 'he'd / Sit like a king there, and like Marat bleed' ('PF', l. 894). Shade, therefore, poses as a monarch, assuming the role of a revolutionary, assassinated by a certain Charlotte (Corday); Kinbote, on the other hand, is assuming the role of a king (Charles), due to be assassinated by a revolutionary Shadow (Gradus).

Such reversals and inversions (of image, role, gender, and wordplay) typify 'the contrapuntal theme' discerned by Shade himself, where what matters most is 'not text, but texture' ('PF', ll. 807–8); or, as Kinbote professes to see it, 'it is the underside of the weave that entrances the beholder and only begetter, whose own past intercoils there with the fate of the innocent author' (*PF* 16). Page Stegner, writing in 1966, had emphasized the 'kaleidoscopic configuration' in *Pale Fire*, which he likened to 'contrapuntal lines of Baroque music'.[24]

The nuances of the title(s) resonate through the work on a profusion of levels.[25] Shade's 'Pale Fire' is barely a pallid glow of the Zemblan epic anticipated by Kinbote; or, perhaps, as is frequently suggested as a central Nabokovian metaphor, this life is but a pale fire compared to that of the next world. Shade's parenthesized couplet, '(But *this* transparent thingum does require / Some moondrop title. Help me, Will! *Pale Fire*.)' ('PF', ll. 961–2), does confirm that he at least knew what he was about when titling his poem; what is less certain is Kinbote's authorship of the overall title (however, such would be the obvious inference if the 'true' designation of the book were to be thought of as '*Pale Fire: A Poem in Four Cantos*, Edited with a Commentary by Charles Kinbote'). The title, given the *Timon of Athens* 'thievery' derivation, is indeed emblematic of the main action – on the literary plane, of course, in particular. On the Timonic ladder of inspirational or textual thievery, linking life to Shakespeare (and others), to Shade, down to Kinbote (or sun, moon, and then sea), Kinbote occupies the lowest rung or, as put by Stephen Parker, '[o]ne man has taken another man's art for his own personal reality. And that, as Nabokov always maintained, is unpardonable'.[26] To return to the opening parallel drawn with James's *The Aspern Papers*, which also concerns the attempted appropriation of literary papers by a manic researcher, Kinbote can be classed as the ultimate 'publishing scoundrel'.[27]

Pale Fire leaves many further as yet unanswered questions. Why is John Shade's middle name 'Francis'? Why is Kinbote obsessed with a car called a 'Kramler': a combination of

Chrysler and Daimler, perhaps?[28] What, if anything, is to be made of Kinbote's allegedly 'remarkable book of surnames', published 'Oxford, 1956' (*PF* 210)?[29] What is the intended satirical target of Shade's 'I.P.H.' ('Institute of Preparation For the Hereafter': 'PF', ll. 502–4)? What notice, if any, should be taken of Nabokov's claim, outside the text (*SO* 74), that Kinbote committed suicide 'after putting the last touches to his edition of the poem' – indeed even 'before completing his Index' (*B Am* 709, n. 6)?[30]

Pale Fire, in addition to being a fable of literary thievery, is a shimmering sequence of doublings ('doublegangers') and identity problems. It is a refracted fantasia of the past in which, in Shade's words, 'resemblances are the shadows of differences' (*PF* 208), and an intellectualized murder story (who exactly murders whom, and why? who is shielding – or 'shading' – whom in the finale? *PF* 231), constructed as an unlikely commentary to a rambling poem. For all its idiosyncrasies and enigmas, one thing can be held as certain: that the whole of *Pale Fire* greatly exceeds the sum of its parts. As we wonder, with Kinbote, at 'the miracle of a few written signs being able to contain immortal imagery' (*PF* 227) and fumble in our attempts to explicate *Pale Fire*, we ourselves, as commentators, must remain ever alive to the inestimable dangers of 'creeping Kinbotism'.[31]

7

Ardor in Ardis: *Ada*

Molchala dver'. I pered vsemi The door stayed silent, and for all to see
muchitel'no ia prolil semia writing with agony I spilled my seed
i ponial vdrug, chto ia v adu. and knew abruptly that I was in Hell.

(V. Nabokov, *Lilit/*'Lilith', Berlin, 1928: *PP* 54–5)

Intelligent readers will abstain from examining this impersonal fantasy for any links with my later fiction. (Ibid. 55)

Ada or Ardor, subtitled 'A Family Chronicle', is indeed a lengthy and extravagant pastiche of that novelistic genre, taking its lead in the opening sentence from an emblematically and inexactly translated quotation from *Anna Karenina* (and its famous opening sentence), held up as the archetypal Russian family chronicle and extended society tale. *Ada* is one of Nabokov's novels of adultery, but it is much more his novel of (sibling) incest, and is the most erotic of his works. It is also the longest and the most ostentatious of his novels, in terms of multilingual wordplay (English, Russian, and French with regularity, and occasional snatches of German and Italian) and multicultural allusion. It therefore demands serious attention. As a mature work, published in 1969, it has presented itself as a major target to Nabokov's detractors, who accuse him of self-indulgence, class and cultural élitism, sexism, and super-arrogance.

And indeed there is much in *Ada* to provide ammunition for such a critique. The main characters, and many of the subordinate characters for that matter, effect intellectual and social imperiousness, exhibiting an impossible and insufferable articulateness and erudition: in the form of trilingual precocity as children, through adult superciliousness, to geriatric *hauteur* (so much so that even their creator disliked them: see *SO* 120, 146). However, once again, nothing in a Nabokov novel is straightforward, and those readers able to control their irritation through the opening pages and sections (some commentators advise skimming, or even skipping, the first three chapters of 'prologue'), and those with sufficient patience and a disposition for re-reading, are ultimately rewarded with a richly patterned feast.

Supreme achievement, or flawed masterpiece? His best writing, or a semi-pornographic longevity fantasy? More than any Nabokov novel, *Ada* may provoke abandonment in its early stages, while its full effects are only to be felt, as *Ada*'s leading interpreter Brian Boyd has stressed, 'through the corrective effects of successive readings'.[1] Linguistic contortion, esoteric erudition, and allusion (intra- and intertextual, as well as interdisciplinary): complexities of Joycean dimensions are frequently suggested.

So, more exactly, what sort of a beast is *Ada or Ardor: A Family Chronicle*? The very title of itself contains more than an inkling. The name 'Ada' (from 'Adelaida') is pronounced, within its inner 'family chronicle' circle at least ('with two deep dark "*a*"s': *A* 37), to rhyme with 'ardor'. The latter feeling is phonically and emotionally connected with 'Ardis' (Hall, or Manor), the Edenic setting of the chronicle's early years ('ardis', meaning 'arrow-head' in Greek, points suggestively to the dominant theme of time). In Russian, *ada* is the genitive form of the word for hell (*ad*) – appropriately enough, as Ada, like her lover Van, we learn (*pace* the family tree as printed immediately after the novel's dedication), had sprung from the loins of Demon Veen. As if that were insufficient, Ada is a homonym too for the Russian '*a, da!*', a Molly Bloom-like 'oh, yes!': to Van, to love, and to life.

In addition to its function as a travesty of the family chronicle, then, *Ada* amounts to a parodic survey-novel of European literature: the Romantics (in particular Chateaubriand and Byron), the Russians (Pushkin, Gogol, Lermontov, and Tolstoy), Flaubert and Proust all come within its purview, with play being made on specific poems by Marvell ('The Garden') and Rimbaud ('Mémoire'), and sideswipes taken at a number of the many figures looked upon by Nabokov with disfavour (Maupassant, Eliot, Pasternak, Freud, Einstein: need we go on?). The Ardis mansion itself is introduced as appearing 'on the gentle eminence of old novels' (*A* 34). In particular, the novel appears designed to demonstrate the incestuousness of literary development; the protagonists' first youthful intimacy takes place in the appropriate setting of the Ardis library. Purporting to be – or masquerading as – Van and Ada Veen's memoirs, *Ada* can also, however, be seen, or has been seen, as merely Van's senile ramblings and distortions, a Proustian novel of time, a two-world neo-Romantic or Symbolist novel (of Antiterra and Terra, however they are to be interpreted), a work of science fiction, and a decadent novel in the *fin-de-siècle* vogue (imbued with 1960s permissiveness, or a veneer of soft-porn burlesque). It may well be many, if not quite all, of these things: it certainly is a cumulative re-elaboration of near enough all Nabokov's earlier themes and techniques.

Ada, at face value at least, is the record of the 97-year-old Van Veen's love affair with his sister (first presented as cousin, and conceivably half-sister), Ada Veen, over an eighty-year period, stretching from what is proffered as the penultimate decade of the nineteenth century and set in a version of the world in which America seems to have been colonized by bilingual Amer-Russians (fluent also, of course, in French – the influence of 'Canady'). Their parental prehistory involves twin sisters (Aqua and Marina) marrying a pair of first cousins (Demon and Daniel Veen), plus a mysterious birth and a recognition scene so precipitate that, as Boyd says, it 'upends all the rules' (*B Am* 546– 7). Anachronisms and unfamiliar geography soon set the reader wondering, as do occasional annotations from Ada herself. The 'now' of the novel is that of the nonagenarian couple composing their chronicle in bed; the rest is memory, spliced with art, dream, and embedded texts. The main emphasis falls on the erotic idyll of their early teenage Ardis summers (beginning impassionately with Van aged 14 and Ada 12), and of the undermining and loss – through infidelity, jealousy, and the march of time – of this Arcadian perfumed garden. The purpose of the chronicle seems to be the regaining of lost paradise – not by physical return, but through art and memory, by process of the patterned reassemblage of story-segment, image, and motif. By the time we reach 'Vaniada's end' (*A* 457; 'the amusing VANIADA' had also been a formulation achieved in Scrabble by Lucette, back in 1888: *A* 178), the overall tapestry, with its implicit interwoven meanings, assumes a greater complexity, and makes a more profound impression, than its supposed authors – for all their intellectual brilliance – may be supposed to have intended.

Ada is constructed in five parts, in a ratio contrarily retrogressive in length to the advance of time. Part 1, covering the opening prologizing sections and the two golden amorous summers ('Ardis One' and 'Ardis Two') of 1884 and 1888 (with brief episodes in between), at 249 pages (in the Penguin edition), comprises over half the book. Part 2, centring on the reunion of 1892, is 93 pages. Part 3, dealing with the events of 1901 and 1905, takes up 66 pages. Part 4, 25 pages long, dovetails the pivotal episode of 1922 (when Van and Ada reunite for good) with ruminations for Van's treatise *The Texture of Time*. Part 5, at a mere 17 pages, brings the action (such as it by now is) up to 1967, thus flying over 45 years. Time, or 'the ardis of Time' (*A* 422), certainly does fly as the novel progresses, and it may be that an analysis based on temporal philosophy, and/or an accommodating slide rule, might reveal the approximation of the chronological structure of *Ada* to its protagonist's (after all, Antiterran?) theorizing. Like Fyodor in *The Gift*, Van lives in hope of 'catching sight of the lining of time' (*A* 178). On the other hand, in one sense contradicting Van's theory, the practice of *Ada* is to be episodic, to recreate and emphasize the key dates and scenes, rather than 'the dim intervals between the dark beats' (*A* 430).

The Texture of Time, or at least tentative drafts towards this treatise, thus intrudes into Part 4. Other embedded texts, or often summaries or descriptions of such, appear elsewhere: letters, notes, poems, and translations; lectures and other works by Van; his novella, *Letters from Terra*, and its much later unauthorized cinematic travesty; fiction written by the Ardis governess Mlle Larivière, and the film *Don Juan's Last Fling* (based on a Larivière novella, and in which Ada's supporting role – albeit unwittingly – seals the fate of the novel's third main character, the Veens' half-sister Lucette). A number of these take on a *mise en abyme* quality as they interknit with the overall texture of *Ada*.[2]

To develop here just one example, by the time of 'Ardis Two' (1888), Ada's amorous life has taken on complications: 'She was like the girl in a film he would see soon, who is in the triple throes of a tragedy which she must conceal lest she lose her only

88

true love, the head of the arrow, the point of the pain' (*A* 152). The 'ardis' or arrow reference, of course, points to Van, while 'pain', by Part 5, becomes synonymous with time. A few pages on and a film starring Marina is being planned. Querying the motivation of the cinematic intrigue, she is told that her 'lover number one', 'Renny, or what's his name, René', as 'it's only a half-hearted flashback...does not know, of course, that she is trying to get rid of lover number two, while she's wondering all the time if she can go on dating number three, the gentleman farmer' (*A* 159). This is to be the film that Van 'would see soon'. The situation parallels exactly the present predicament of Ada (and that of Marina in the past); 'René' (deriving from Chateaubriand) is a pet-name of Ada's for Van in 1884. The film itself is an adaptation of the governess Mlle Larivière's novel *Les enfants maudits* (1887, which 'finally degenerated' into *The Young and the Doomed*, 1890: *A* 333), written under the pen-name 'Guillaume de Monparnasse' and possibly owing something, as well as to Maupassant, Chateaubriand, and the goings-on at Ardis (Larivière had informed Lucette that 'the beautiful ARDIS meant "the point of an arrow"'": *A* 177), to another literary governess (she from *The Turn of the Screw*). Additionally, flashback – or perhaps 'half-hearted flashback' – is, it will by now be understood, an overriding technique of *Ada*.

The essential narrative presentation of *Ada* mimics the traditional styles, devices, and types 'portrayed in extravagant romances and senile memoirs' (*A* 172), with reinvented dialogue and retrospective interior monologue. It thus appears to comprise Van Veen's composition, that of an old man looking back (although himself still susceptible to 'the ardis of Time'), with occasional marginal comments or quibbles from Ada. Now and then, however, she is prevailed upon to take over the narrative herself, whereupon Van's often baroque style may give way to a positively rococo variation by Ada:

> Go on from here, Ada, please.
>
> (She). Billions of boys. Take one fairly decent decade. A billion of Bills, good, gifted, tender and passionate, not only spiritually but physically well-meaning Billions, have bared the jillions of their no less tender and brilliant Jills during that decade, at stations and

89

under conditions that have to be controlled and specified by the worker, lest the entire report be choked up by the weeds of statistics and waist-high generalizations. (*A* 60)

It is Ada who at that point coins for the pair the phrase 'unique super-imperial couple', and it seems impossible to judge the extent to which the entire saga is a joint opus,[3] let alone its detailed reliability, when Ada intervenes with:

(Van, I trust your taste and your talent but are we *quite sure* we should keep reverting so *zestfully* to that wicked world which after all may have existed only oneirologically, Van? Marginal note in Ada's 1965 hand; crossed out lightly in her latest wavering one.) (*A* 19)

'Memory met imagination halfway in the hammock of his boyhood's dawns', writes Van, in a not dissimilar vein (*A* 59). As early as the second Ardis summer of 1888, we are told, great pains were taken to attempt to recapture every last detail of the summer of 1884. It seems as though *Ada* was already and even then in the making, in what was to amount to a constant process of reminiscence, juxtaposition ('sudden juxtapositions that revived the part while vivifying the whole': *A* 31), reconstruction, and synthesis. The actual writing of the chronicle, though, purports to be carried out through various stages of composition and revision between 1957 and 1967. 'Ought to begin dating every page of the manuscript: Should be kinder to my unknown dreamers' (*A* 99), runs a post-1960 gloss by Van.

The tone of much of the declamation employed by the narrator(s), with its compulsive (often bilingual or trilingual) punning and double entendre, its use of paronomasia, alliteration ('the pre-tunnel toot of the two-two to Toulouse': *A* 85), assonance, anagrams ('Eros, the rose and the sore': *A* 288), neologisms, and other verbal effects, together with its ornate meshwork of cultural reference, amounts to a kind of upmarket version of *skaz* narration, a narrative form identified by the Russian Formalists in works by Gogol and others as a posed (traditionally often substandard or quirky) narrational discourse that departs from what may be assumed to be primary authorial linguistic register. Even late Nabokov, in his other fictional and non-fictional works and (premeditated) interviews, did not consistently write or speak in quite this manner, as the briefest glance at his autobiography, *Speak, Memory,* or his next novel, *Transparent Things,* will confirm. The *fabula* and *siuzhet* divergence remarked on in *Pale Fire* appears far less radical in *Ada,* not surprisingly, perhaps, given its ostensible family-chronicle design. Nevertheless, the chronological structuring remarked on above points up the profuse emphasis here on *siuzhet* in all its rhapsodic detail.

Further unusual editorial and paratextual features also need to be borne in mind. The official (and deliberately misleading) version of a 'Family Tree' has already been mentioned;[4] this is counted as a part of the text itself (as opposed to, for instance, familiar translations of *War and Peace,* to which a 'cast of characters' may be provided by an editor or translator). To whom it should be attributed is less certain: whether to the putative author(s) of the text or to another figure, the manuscript's 'Editor'. This personage is assumed to be a Mr Ronald Oranger – on the basis of an almost epigraphic note that precedes the opening page of Part 1 (and, in some editions, the novel's title): 'With the exception of Mr and Mrs Ronald Oranger, a few incidental figures, and some non-American citizens, all the persons mentioned by name in this book are dead. [Ed.]'. This editor has had, or perhaps has seized (Kinbote- and 'publishing scoundrel'-like) control over final presentation of the text, as his own occasional interventions prove.[5] 'Mrs Ronald Oranger' is the text's typist, the Veens' last secretary, employed by them under her maiden name of Violet Knox. Oranger, whose competence may be as doubtful as his role is mysterious, has left within the text – and at a supremely vital point of the action at that – such an intrusive authorial instruction as: 'Although Lucette had never died before – no, *dived* before, Violet – from such a height' (*A* 389).

The preliminary editorial note also appears to prove that the authors ('Ada. Van. Ada. Vaniada. Nobody.': *A* 457) have indeed, by the time of publication, themselves died into the text, 'as it were, *into* the finished book, into Eden or Hades, into the prose of the book or the poetry of its blurb' (*A* 460). And indeed, the 'blurb', somewhat irregularly and by whomsoever it may be supposed to have been written (whether by Van, or by Ada, or conceivably by Oranger himself), now concludes the text of *Ada* (*A* 460–1). It ostensibly presents the novel as a good read in the mode of popular fiction ('In spite of the many intricacies of plot and psychology, the story proceeds at a spanking pace', etc.: *A* 460), while simultaneously contriving to tie up details of its own concealed patterns of imagery in its brief final paragraph. This blurb itself, in the event, achieved transposition into genuine paratext by being featured on the dustjacket of the 1969 English edition of *Ada* (presumably with Nabokov's approval). In another sense, it may be seen to balance the three opening sections of prologue.

One further paratextual quirk yet remained up Nabokov's sleeve, however, as he was to add to the first Penguin edition of 1971 '"Notes to Ada" by Vivian Darkbloom' (*A* 463–77). The androgynous 'Darkbloom', we may recall, is a minor character (Quilty's mistress and his biographer) from *Lolita*, and an anagram of the ultimate author. These notes supply certain missing translations and identify some allusions (a sop to hostile reviewers and an encouragement to future readers?), but, although not quite in the class of Kinbote's 'Index' to *Pale Fire*, they are seen as less full or helpful than they might have been.[6]

As far as reactions to *Ada* are concerned, much is likely to hang on the attitude of readers to the novel's eccentric setting. Tricks of history (Russians in America, the annexation of France by England, a prohibition on the use of electricity after some unspecified disaster, and a variety of technological quirks) are attributed to the chronicle's *mise-en-scène* – the world of Antiterra (sometimes referred to as 'Demonia'). Antiterran history is, on average, about half a century ahead of our own (though what was admittedly the second Crimean War, for instance, starts only in 1888); such writers as Pushkin and Tolstoy seem to occupy a familiar literary place; Chekhov has written *The Four Sisters*, while works by Joyce, Proust, and others too are known within the nineteenth century. A writer called 'Osberg' (a scrambling of 'Borges') has written an erotic novel (*La Gitanilla*) that seems to be associated with what we know as *Lolita*. Most things are somewhat skewed: names, dates, gadgets, literary figures, and works. Some of these distortions are glossed by Darkbloom's 'Notes'; others are left for the reader to work out. All of this may be regarded either as an attraction of, or a distraction from, the discourse of *Ada*.

Vague intimations, rumours, or hallucinations are mooted of an alternative world called Terra, the history of which seems to match that of Earth. Van Veen, whose supposed mother Aqua had been much taken with 'all the fangles of cranks and Christians' (*A* 23), was to devote much of his career in psychology to a study of this phenomenon.

> Revelation can be more perilous than Revolution. Sick minds identified the notion of a Terra planet with that of another world and this 'Other World' got confused not only with the 'Next World' but with the Real World in us and beyond us. (*A* 23)

Terra, then, may belong to a parallel universe or represent an afterlife; it may be myth, 'specular...phenomenon' (*A* 21), 'random variation' (*A* 328), or 'sibling planet' (*A* 181), or amount to an alternative perspective, or to no more than 'jagged bits filched from deranged brains' (*A* 271). The coupling of Antiterra and Terra has caused Ada to be read as science fiction; Antiterra, as the nineteenth century out of joint, has also been seen as an extreme form of defamiliarization (the Formalist device of *ostranenie*).[7] If so, it is stretched to the point of magical realism.

While most commentators appear to take Antiterra at face value, there are at least a small number who do not. Bobbie Ann Mason declares Antiterra to be Van Veen's fantasy and the sibling planets a reflection of the incest theme – Van's escape into a distorted solipsism.[8] Charles Nicol, in a challenging and neglected essay from 1982, is convinced that 'the façade of Antiterra can be torn away', exposing Van Veen as a narrator of monumental unreliability and mnemonic distortion, resulting from a deliberate confusion of life with dream (the Villa Venus sequence) and art (here, literature and painting), laced with defiance and frayed by senility: 'Memory replaces life with art.'[9] Nicol believes time in *Ada* to have been effectively frozen at the pivotal date of 1922, with a consequent retrogressive refraction of anachronisms and delusions. An in-depth investigation of the displacements in *Ada*, he speculates, 'might completely overturn the tangled family relationships of the novel, and establish a radically different picture' (*5th Arc*, 240). A further corollary of such a picture, were one to be established, might be, one could further conjecture, not only a recognition of 'Antiterra' and 'Terra' as some sort of a solipsistic bisection, but a requirement for an alternative ('realistic') explanation for Van Veen's cultural background. He would emerge, it might be conjectured, as something of a (rampantly heterosexual!) Kinbote figure, a demented representative of the first Russian emigration, traumatized by lost childhood, lost love, and a lost world: not, though, a representative of Nabokov's own generation, but displaced to that of his father (born, like Van Veen, in 1870; assassinated in 1922).

Let us now turn, however, to what may be the most central of many questions arising from *Ada*, even – or especially – when read at face value. Why, given the permissive lifestyle of Antiterran high society and Veen family history, and his own outrageous libertinism, is Demon Veen so shocked by the incestuous relationship of Van and Ada? Why is there no return to Ardis? Why, given the sexual depredations he visits upon almost all other remotely eligible females, and the obvious attraction she holds for him, does Van adamantly refuse to make love with Lucette? Or perhaps these are really reducible, in whatever order they may be posed, to just one question.

D. Barton Johnson has meticulously traced what he calls 'the labyrinth of incest' in *Ada*, both through its literary sources and within the Zemski–Veen family tree, concluding that 'the incestuous relationship of Van and Ada is but the final episode in a series of incestuous matings among Veens and Zemskis over several generations'.[10] In particular, Demon and Daniel Veen may be twins and may have a half or even full sibling relationship with Aqua and Marina. While there may be no solid evidence of father–daughter incest through the inter-twining branches of this family 'tree of knowledge', there is certainly tentative textual and sexual suggestion surrounding the Veen daughters in their Ardis idyll.

The Ardis estate, even before the first 'fall', is depicted (retrospectively, of course) displaying the following natural feature: 'Overhead the arms of a linden stretched toward those of an oak, like a green-spangled beauty flying to meet her strong father hanging by his feet from the trapeze. Even then did we both understand that kind of heavenly stuff, even then.' As Ada sees it, '[t]he teil is the flying Italian lady, and the old oak aches, the old lover aches, but still catches her every time' – or, if not exactly that, 'she did say something extravagant, something quite out of keeping with her tender age' (*A* 46). When sibling incest does get under way, Van cannot decide of Ada 'whether she really was utterly ignorant and as pure as the night sky... or whether total experience advised her to indulge in a cold game' (*A* 95). On an 1888 visit to Ardis, Demon stops himself telling Van something (what Van already knows, or more?), presumably of family relationships – '[s]ome day it would have to be said' (*A* 191) – and proceeds to 'kissing [Ada] in the neck, in the hair, burrowing in her sweetness with more than an uncle's fervor' (*A* 193). And, perhaps, more than a father's? Other instances of Demon's attentions to Ada are plentiful, and subsequently, in the years of separation following Ardis Two, both 'watchful fools' and long-standing friends were speaking of Demon as 'Van's successor' (*A* 308). The apparent dismissal of this by the chroniclers ('actually, he was getting more and more occupied with Spanish girls': *A* 308) is not necessarily to be fully trusted.

'Demonia' is an occasional alternative appellation for Antiterra, and 'demonism' there is rife, as Demon appears to rule the roost (until his demise in an aviation disaster). A parodic Lucifer figure, traduced from Lermontov's narrative poem, *The Demon*, Dementiy (Demon) Veen, with his wings (either figurative or literal) and his simulated youthfulness (displayed in his portrait by Vrubel: *A* 398), casts a long shadow. Van quotes, purportedly from a bad translation of the pseudonymous Monparnasse's 'rather comic tale' being travestied into film: 'The infamous shadow of our unnatural affair will follow us into the low depths of the Inferno which our Father who is in the sky shows to us with his superb digit' (*A* 170). Demon duly raises his finger to put an end to the frolics of his progeny, at least for another thirteen years and thereafter a further seventeen, whether to mask his own incestuous involvement or, in a belated – and, in the event, forlorn – attempt, to safeguard his already grossly inbred line.

Neither is Daniel Veen, Demon's ineffectual art-dealing counterpart-cousin or brother, by any means beyond suspicion. For Ada's twelfth birthday, her supposed father had bought her 'a huge beautiful doll – unfortunately, and strangely, more or less naked' (*A* 70). Ada's response, termed by her mother 'I don't know – satanic!', is to suggest he 'carry the whole business to the surgical dump'; almost immediately, Ada, playing a game of 'anagrams', from 'insect' proclaims the word 'incest' (*A* 71). Lucette, too, has had cause to complain of her father (Dan) being 'the silent-explorer type' (*A* 366).

Demon does not, however, 'give a damn whether or not you slept with Lucette', as he writes to Van after her suicide (*A* 391). His sole concern lies with Ada, her life and career. Aqua (Van's surrogate mother), his wet nurse and 'all the fond, all the frail' coming into close contact with Van, 'as later Lucette did, to give another example', were doomed 'to know anguish and calamity, unless strengthened by a strain of his father's demon blood' (*A* 22–3). In other words, only Ada is immune: she ('Adochka') is, of course, *'adova dochka* (Hell's daughter)' (*A* 317), just as Van himself is a 'Vandemonian' (*A* 296). The adulterous side of Demonia is 'Desdemonia' (*A* 408), but this is a planet, Van writes to Ada, on which 'Lucettes are doomed' (*A* 391) to demonic and venereal neglect, their looks and their incisive wit notwithstanding. 'Mixed metaphors and double-talk became all three Veens, the children of Venus,' we are told (*A* 323), while Van himself ranks Lucette's crack over Mademoiselle Condor '(nasalizing the first syllable)' as the '[b]est Franco-English pun I've ever heard' (*A* 378). As Johnson observes, Lucette is 'the loser in the incestuous triangle "Lucette–Van–Ada" as is Aqua in her own triangle "Aqua–Demon–Marina"'.[11] In incest, ultimately two is company and three is a crowd.

Ada and Lucette have performed together to each other's satisfaction in Van's absence (if not with great success with him as a threesome). So, why not Van and Lucette? Van is lethally jealous of Ada's affairs with other men, but much less so with regard to women. Ada, for her part, is unconcerned with Van's conquests and cavortings, but cautious, to say the least, when it comes to Lucette. 'Perhaps she excites you? Yes? She excites you, confess?', she suggests when the 12-year-old Lucette has been caressed as a decoy tactic (Ardis Two: *A* 169). 'She's an utterly mad and depraved gipsy nymphet, of course', she affirms the same summer (*A* 180), transferring to Lucette her own future (and indeed, for her sister, indirectly fatal) role in *Don Juan's Last Fling*, as appropriated from the Osberg novel. Suspecting Van of deception (and, ironically, without justification in this instance) involving 'Miss Condor' on the *Admiral Tobakoff* liner, Lucette declares '*tu sais que j'en vais mourir*', and means it (*A* 380). Ada echoes the same phrase later at Van's protests over her staying with her sick husband Andrey, but doesn't mean it. As Demon is about to discover Ada living in Van's flat (1892), Van mouths an ineffectual '*je ne suis pas seul*' (*A* 342); the Russian version of this ('*Ya ne odin*': *A* 387) is Van's last, fatal, and invented response to Lucette by telephone, to keep her out of his *Tobakoff* cabin.

After the abortive three-way romp of 1892, Ada had admitted to being 'really jealous' of Lucette 'for the first time in my fire [thus in the manuscript for "life." Ed.] Van, Van, somewhere, some day, after a sunbath or dance, you will sleep with her, Van!' (*A* 332). Nine years later, on the *Tobakoff* with Lucette and in a highly charged atmosphere of erotic repartee, Van manages to refrain from this after sunbathing, and successfully avoids the 'ballroom dance competition' (*A* 382), but has decided after all to succumb finally to 'the free, new, apricot fire of anticipation' (*A* 384) when Ada makes her ravishing screen appearance as the gipsy Dolores in *Don Juan's Last Fling*. Ada, as *dea ex* (cinematic) *machina*, thus saves the day, driving Van to rush off to effect masturbatory relief (twice, to make double sure!), while Lucette allows herself to be detained by boring aquaintances; his subsequent untrue telephonic excuse for not receiving her after all propels Lucette into her oceanic dive.

For all the remaining sixty-five years (covered in just seventy pages), *The Texture of Time*, and the denial that even Part 5 is meant as an epilogue (though admitted as a 'true introduction', *A* 445), the novel, arguably, is effectively over with the death of Lucette (just as *Anna Karenina* effectively concludes with the suicide of Anna). What remains is the drawn-out and laborious procedure and confirmation of its composition. And yet, what of 'the Ardors and Arbors of Ardis – ... the leitmotif rippling through *Ada*' (*A* 460)?

Unexpectedly as far as Lucette is concerned, Ardis has been left to her by Marina.

> 'Look, Van,' she said (finishing her fourth flute). 'Why not risk it? Everything is quite simple. You marry me. You get my Ardis. We live there, you write there. I keep melting into the background, never bothering you. We invite Ada – alone, of course – to stay for a while on *her* estate, for I had always expected mother to leave Ardis to her. (*A* 366)

This may be the champagne talking, and marrying a half-sister may be no easier than marrying a full one; however, asked a few days later on the *Tobakoff* where she thought she was going: 'To Ardis, with him – came the prompt reply – for ever and ever' (*A* 374). The sun-terrace of the liner is referred to as 'Eden'; diving into the pool, Lucette 'prepared to ardis into the amber' (*A* 376–7). Having premeditated drastic action in anticipation of failure in seducing Van, Lucette apparently regards 'Ardis' by now as either paradise or doom. The estate is soon doomed anyway, described in Ada's letter, semi-coded to pass the scrutiny of her formidable sister-in-law, Dasha, as 'the lost castle of poor Lucette's and happy, happy Adette's childhood, now a "home for Blind Blacks" – both my mother and L., I'm sure, would have backed Dasha's advice to turn it over to her Sect' (*A* 394). Ardis Hall has passed on, just as the Ardis idyll has long since receded into the past. Only sixty years later, collaborating on the chronicle, does Ada come round to what had been Lucette's way of thinking:

> 'Oh, Van, oh Van, we did not love her enough. *That's* whom you should have married,...and then everything would have been all right – I would have stayed with you both in Ardis Hall, and instead of that happiness, handed out gratis, instead of all that we *teased* her to death!' (*A* 459)

As Van and Ada continue to be haunted by the memory of Lucette, Ardis could neither be physically revisited nor emotionally reconquered. It could only be artistically recreated, to give it the meaning it either had, might have had, or should have had.

The photographs taken over the Ardis One and Two summers, with which Kim (the former Ardis kitchen boy turned professor of graphic arts) blackmails Ada, offend Van less on moral grounds than as aesthetic sabotage. Photographic realism does not measure up to the creative process of life, memory, and art required for the Veen version of family chronicle. Even the extravagant silver-screen fantasy of *Don Juan's Last Fling*, with its 'glorious torture' (for Van, if for no one else) embodied in Ada's fleeting performance, constitutes 'a complete refutation of odious Kim's odious stills' (*A* 393). The action has to be imaginatively reinstated 'against the green moving backdrop of one of our Ardis sets', where as 'lovers *and* siblings', cries Ada, 'we have a double chance of being together in eternity, in terrarity. Four pairs of eyes in paradise!' (*A* 456).

Kim's photographic vision is anathema to Van Veen's perception and has to be exorcised and excised:

> 'Art my *foute*. This is the hearse of *ars*, a toilet roll of the Carte du Tendre! I'm sorry you showed it to me. That ape has vulgarized our own mind-pictures. I will either horsewhip his eyes out or redeem our childhood by making a book of it: *Ardis*, a family chronicle.' (*A* 320)

'On second thoughts, I will not write that Family Chronicle' (*A* 321), adds Van. Ultimately, it seems, assuming we believe the 'forkings and continuations that occur to the dream-mind' (*A* 351), both threats are carried out. Kim is consigned to 'a nice Home for Disabled Professional People' (the 'Home for Blind Blacks'?). The Villa Venus brothels, ostensibly the dream product of another branch of Veens, flourished only temporarily as 'parodies of paradise' (*A* 275). Driven to recreate paradise, and to need Eden, Van and Ada eventually do ape Ardis through 'ample and delightful chronicle' (*A* 460).

Ada has been read as a morality lesson by Mason, who sees in it an escape mechanism for Van to appease his incestuous guilt; but Boyd, more credibly, prefers to consider it a chronicle of selfishness, emphasizing through its covert patterning the base treatment by the two principals of their half-sister Lucette. While this approach, enhanced by Boyd's exegetic mastery, has rather more to commend it, and Lucette inspires some of Nabokov's finest writing, one may nevertheless incline to side with Johnson's view that 'the meaning of *Ada*'s sibling incest theme is to be sought in the world of art rather than in the world of ideas', with *Ada* 'the consequence of a complex act of incestuous procreation'.[12] Pekka Tammi describes *Ada* as 'a veritable development *ad absurdum* of the structural principle canonized' in *Speak, Memory*.[13] The text of *Ada* is sprinkled with Nabokovian self-reference: such anagrammatic personages occur as Baron Klim Avidov and Ben Sirine ('Been Sirin'),[14] as well as the appended Vivian Darkbloom, while *Lolita*, *Pale Fire* (and John Shade), 'Spring in Fialta', 'The Vane Sisters', and several other works are invoked. As a transformed reconstruction of the Nabokovian world, the cultures and languages of Russia, Europe, and 'a dream-bright America' (*A* 460), *Ada*, as Boyd has averred, 'sums up everything that mattered to Nabokov' (*B Am* 510), and it stands as the most ambitious and imaginative of his posed, or transposed, (auto)biographies.

8

Looking at the Harlequins

Look at the Harlequins! (1974) was Nabokov's last completed novel, and it may be fitting in a number of ways that it has to be seen as his last fictional bow. G. M. Hyde adjudges that whereas '*Transparent Things* had the air of an epilogue, this novel is a kind of fictionalized index to Nabokov's work'; furthermore, he states, this 'positively last performance' (although, as he was writing, Hyde expected that '[d]espite the gestures of finality in the last two novels there will surely be others') 'shows beyond doubt that all Nabokov's works are really one work'.[1] This point of view is hard to dispute, in that Nabokov's last published novel is surely the *last* Nabokov novel that any would-be reader of Nabokov should read first.

'Look at the harlequins!', an instruction issued in the early pages of the novel, assumes the quality of a maxim not only for this work as a whole, but for Nabokov's *œuvre* in totality; it is reduced to the acronym 'LATH' in the text itself, and this is the shorthand title adopted in subsequent criticism. Even more than Nabokov's previous novels, if that may be thought possible, *LATH* combines and confuses fiction with biography, biography with autobiography, one world of fictional reality with another, and invention (or delusion) with memory. Auto-intertextuality, at a variety of levels, is certainly the name of one of the principal games. Allusions are made, and names, motifs, or details appropriated (often in disguised or skewed form), in particular from *The Real Life of Sebastian Knight*, *Lolita*, *Ada*, *The Gift*, and *Glory*; and, more fleetingly, from many another work. Of special importance, lurking in the background as declared autobiography, is *Speak, Memory*, as well as details – tacit or otherwise –

from Nabokov's personal biography.[2] The ensuing gamut of elements – of pastiche, metafiction, the blurring of boundaries, and confusions of identity – should make *LATH*, as David Rampton suggests, 'the ideal Nabokov novel for the post-modernist critic' (providing always that [s]he knows all, or enough, of the previous works!); yet the resulting prominence of the author will give pause to some, who may prefer to cling to the 'death of the author' as a credo.[3] Conversely, any purely Formalist-structuralist analysis would certainly be problematic.

The first startling sign (missed by some first-timers) hits the reader from the paratext. Following the title page and the customary dedication (though here possessing a special significance) 'To Véra', we find a list of 'Other Books by the Narrator'. These titles (six 'in Russian' and six 'in English') bear a clear (or in some cases a less than clear) resemblance, with a slight additional chronological displacement, to the names of works by Nabokov. Thus we find *'Tamara 1925'* (Nabokov's fictional name in *Speak, Memory* for his first serious love), rather than *Mashen'ka* (or *Mary*, 1926). *'Pawn Takes Queen 1927'*, we gather, seems an amalgam of *The Luzhin Defense* and *King, Queen, Knave* (1930 and 1928 respectively). *Kamera obskura* (1933, subsequently *Laughter in the Dark*) has become *'Camera Lucida* (Slaughter in the Sun) *1931'*, while *The Gift* (Russian title *Dar*, published in full 1952) is *'The Dare 1950'*. Among the 'English' titles we find *'See under Real 1939'* ('really' *The Real Life of Sebastian Knight, 1941*) and *Dr Olga Repnin 1946* (standing in for the masculine *Pnin*, 1957). *'A Kingdom by the Sea 1962'* takes its title from the line in Poe's 'Annabel Lee', used in *Lolita*, and combines elements of that novel with motifs from *Ada* (1962 coming midway between 1955 and 1969), while *'Ardis 1970'* clearly derives also from *Ada*. Other titles clarify when references to their content occur subsequently in the text; two, however, have no clear equivalent in Nabokov's career: *'Plenilune 1929'*, said to be a verse novel; and a supposed story collection, *'Exile from Mayda 1947'*. Confusion over all these titles, and their subject matter, carries on into the text, where it is shared by most of the characters and occasionally by the narrator himself.

What, then, is going on here? *LATH* purports to be the autobiography, or the memoirs, of a Russian-émigré-turned-English (or rather American) writer called Vadim Vadimovich

N.(?) – here referred to as Vadim or VV – born in 1899, who attended Cambridge, lived in Paris, pursued an academic and literary career in the United States, and then returned to live in Europe, flush with the success of a controversial bestseller. This figure has had 'three or four successive wives' (*LATH* 9) – four, if we assume formalities eventually to have taken place with the last-named 'you' (which may be compared with 'you' from the later pages of *Speak, Memory* and the intermittent mode of addressing Zina in *The Gift*) – and is equally vague about many other things, people, and scenes. 'Dementia is one of the characters of my story' (*LATH* 72), he affirms ('VV' being a formulation recalling, of course, Van Veen, as well as Vladimir Vladimirovich Nabokov); and indeed, he suffers from mental disturbance throughout his life. One bizarre symptom of this, a mental (though for decades not physical) inability to about turn when engaged on imaginary perambulation leads, in 1970, we are told, to an almost fatal breakdown.[4] The present 'moment of writing', we gather (*LATH* 133), is 15 February 1974; Nabokov himself actually completed *LATH* on 3 April 1974 (*GCVN* p. xlix).

So is *LATH* therefore a spoof autobiography? Indeed it is, but, as always, there is rather more to it than that. According to Renate Lachmann autobiography is in any case, 'a parody of one's own self'.[5] Here the effect is more than doubled: it is carried onward almost *ad infinitum*, into what D. Barton Johnson terms 'worlds in regression' (thus titling his 1985 book). As a starting-point, Brian Boyd argues, Nabokov was reacting to the antics of Andrew Field who, in his 1977 and 1986 versions of Nabokov's biography, 'enacted in real life the roles of Nabokov's two invented inept biographers': Mr Goodman of *The Real Life of Sebastian Knight* (who is further castigated as 'Hamlet Godman' in *LATH*) and Kinbote of *Pale Fire* (*B Am* 621). Nabokov therefore determined 'to outfield Field' (Johnson, *GCVN* 330) by creating his own parodic autobiography of the life and works of a manic alter ego figure, 'unwittingly fabricated...from those of "another" writer'. At the same time, in introducing the idealized muse figure of 'you', Nabokov was paying a last fictional tribute to Véra and creating a paean to married love out of the semi-farcical career of Vadim Vadimovich. Many further aspects of the novel, however, remain to be explored: the 'harlequins', the self-referential allusions, the wordplay, and the nature and significance of the dementia require comment, for a start.

'Stop moping!' she would cry: 'Look at the harlequins!'
'What harlequins? Where?'
'Oh, everywhere. All around you. Trees are harlequins, words are harlequins. So are situations and sums. Put two things together – jokes, images – and you get a triple harlequin. Come on! Play! Invent the world! Invent reality!' (*LATH* 13)

The child Vadim immediately follows this injunction of his grand-aunt. Indeed, 'I invented my grand-aunt in honor of my first daydreams,' he somewhat disconcertingly adds. Webster's *New Collegiate Dictionary* (based on that Webster's so famously and thoroughly utilized by Nabokov), deriving 'harlequin' from the Middle French *Helquin*, a demon, cites the 'comedic' character with 'shaved head, masked face, variegated tights, and wooden sword', along with the following usages: 'buffoon', 'a variegated pattern (as of a textile)', and 'a combination of colors in patches on a solid ground (as in the coats of some dogs)'. The 'wooden sword' is effectively a kind of wand, or lath (emblematized by the acronym of the title) and, as we shall see, almost all these other harlequinesque qualities and details resonate through *LATH*.[6] Nabokov's harlequinade extends, we may note, into the natural world, into verbal structure, and into 'situations and sums'. The potential for combination (to make 'a triple harlequin') is equivalent to the young Ada's system of 'things', 'towers', and 'bridges' (*A* 63).

Nabokov privately referred to *LATH* as 'Look at the Masks!' (*B Am* 630), alluding back, as Boyd demonstrates, to his first encounter with Véra at a masked charity ball.[7] A mini-masquerade 'in the low relief of a pantomime' is staged for Vadim's arrival at Villa Iris, with Ivor and Iris pretending that she is deaf and dumb (*LATH* 17). Carried away by the 'iridescent bubbles in [the] alembics' of his first English novel, *See under Real* ('the admirable phenomenon of a bogus *biographie romancée* being gradually supplanted by the true story of a great man's life' – in itself virtually a description of *LATH*), Vadim exclaims 'look at the harlequins, everybody look – Iris, Annette, Bel, Louise, and you, you my ultimate and immortal one' (*LATH* 101).

Here the harlequin masks, ostensibly pertaining to verbal acrobatics, invoke also the list of Vadim's *innamorate*. Such pantomime figures as circus performers (and imagery), actors, acrobats, and ballet dancers abound in what Lucy Maddox calls 'this carnival book', reminding us that the opening scenes are set in the Riviera village of Carnavaux.[8] The combination of Riviera, circus, and portents of doom are reminiscent too of 'Spring in Fialta'. The 'procession of my Russian and English harlequins' (*LATH* 179) comprises both Vadim's books themselves and the cast of characters from them, and, as Maddox says, 'His harlequins in turn mimic the people of Nabokov's books.' Harlequins can also be poets ('my dear bespangled mimes and their wands of painted lath': *LATH* 130), butterflies, and even motels. Vadim's motels prefigure 'the stages of my future travels with my darling daughter' (*LATH* 124), while echoing *Lolita* (by that 'other writer'), a work conjointly emblematized near the end by 'a pair of harlequin sunglasses' (*LATH* 195).

In terms of style, Vadim wishes to produce a harlequinade of prose upon switching to English ('from the fata-morganic prose that I had willed into being in the desert of exile': *LATH* 102). We have 'harlequins', then, rather than 'dummies': a switch 'not to the dead leaden English of the high seas with dummies in sailor suits, but an English I alone would be responsible for, in all its new ripples and changing light' (*LATH* 103). The English of Nabokov is what is required, not that of Conrad.

Self-referential allusion, as we should by now have gathered, is carried on in *LATH* to a far-reaching – some would say extravagant – degree. The opening paragraph of the novel reads almost like a synopsis of *The Gift*, while subsuming too what Boyd terms 'Nabokov's slyly inverted tribute to fate's persistence in bringing himself and Véra together' (*B Am* 630). Conversely, the closing pages of *The Gift*, in which Fyodor and Zina together examine the quirks and manoevres of fate in bringing them together, seem to be re-enacted in *LATH*, as Maddox has pointed out.[9] 'Now isn't that the plot for a remarkable novel? What a theme!' (*G* 331); 'an autobiography', prompts Zina; Fyodor stresses that he would 'shuffle, mix, rechew and rebelch everything', and that it would be years in preparation. The result was not just the novel that we know as

The Gift, but, nearly forty years later, the one we know as *LATH*. Fyodor then proceeds to quote a passage from 'an old French sage' whom he wishes to translate; on sensing the approach of death, the sage 'invited guests to a feast, acrobats, actors, poets, a crowd of dancing girls, three magicians', for 'melodious verses, masks and music' (*G* 332); Fyodor expresses a wish to die in like manner, and Maddox sees *LATH* as fulfilling this wish too, as 'a lively parting feast'.

Vadim's novel *The Dare* seems a parodic variation on *The Gift*; published by the 'Turgenev Publishing House, New York' rather than the Chekhov house of that city, publishers of the first integral *The Gift*. Its 'hero and part-time narrator', Victor, insets into his novel 'on a dare' a biography of Dostoevsky (rather than of Chernyshevsky), 'whose novels he condemns as absurd with their black-bearded killers presented as mere negatives of Jesus Christ's conventional image, and weepy whores borrowed from maudlin romances of an earlier age'; in its final pages Victor, for another dare, walks 'through a perilous forest into Soviet territory' and 'as casually' strolls back (*LATH* 85). This ending thus plays on the end of *Glory*, which Vadim's original mode of emigration has already parodied, as a reverse journey to that of *Glory*'s Martin Edelweiss (see *LATH* 14).

There are abundant allusions to *Lolita* in *LATH*. Nabokov counters the popular supposition that he himself must have had an active interest in nymphets by bestowing such a propensity on Vadim: both his daughter Bel (whom – unaccountably to her, and to her fury – he once calls 'Dolly': *LATH* 154) and Dolly von Borg (surname reminiscent of Borges, or 'Osberg' from *Ada*)[10] adopt Lolita (Dolores/Dolly) roles, and there are name-droppings too of 'Isabel Lee', 'Annabel', and 'Virginia' (as in Poe: *LATH* 134, 146, 170). The blurb quoted on *A Kingdom by the Sea* suggests a scrambling of *Lolita* and *Ada*, and contrasts with the travestied synopsis, apparently of *Lolita*, supplied by the Soviet agent Oleg Orlov (*LATH* 170, 172). Film versions of *Kingdom* and *Lolita* seem to merge in a mention of 'pretty Lola Sloan and her lollypop' (*LATH* 170: suggestive of 'Lolita – Sue Lyon'). Bel goes off with a certain Charlie (the first name of Lolita's boy lover at Camp Q, and here too associated with a children's camp: *LATH* 154, 157). The Mirana Palace hotel (*LATH* 30) revisits Humbert's childhood home, the Hotel Mirana (*L* 10).

'Mirages of motels', a car called a 'Hummer', and 'the dumbest address' ever invented, 'Dumbert Dumbert, Dumberton', combine with a 'humming' Dolly (*LATH* 112, 116), sending an ostentatious signal to even the most casual reader of *Lolita*. 'McNab', the supposed actor (as Ivor Black calls Vadim, *LATH* 12; or 'MacNab', 194), may be reminiscent of 'McFate'; and there is much more.[11]

Ada too has its quota. 'Ada Bredow, a first cousin of mine whom I flirted with disgracefully' one childhood summer, and said to resemble Bel 'in this dismal business of Isabel Lee' (*LATH* 134), is recreated along with that 'avenue of statues and lilacs' in Vadim's 'most private book', *Ardis* (184). One of the Iranian circus women ('like birds of paradise') seen by Vadim on a plane in Soviet Russia was a 'dark-haired pale beauty in black bolero and yellow sharovars who reminded me of Iris or a prototype of Iris' (*LATH* 164); the prototype would seem to be Ada, as seen by Van Veen leaving Ardis the second summer ('a black-haired girl of sixteen or so, in yellow slacks and a black bolero': *A* 233). Vadim claims his own father was nicknamed 'Demon', that he was painted by Vrubel, and that he was used as 'the father of the passionate siblings in the best of my English romaunts, *Ardis* (1970)' (*LATH* 81). More will be said of siblings shortly.

The Real Life of Sebastian Knight has already been indicated as one model for the sort of operation Nabokov is carrying out in *LATH*. The 'mucking biograffitist' Ham Godman (*LATH* 137, 178) has been noted already. At the beginning of *LATH*, Ivor Black hopes for a visit from Sebastian ('whoever that was': *LATH* 11), while Nina Lecerf is said to be a neighbour (18). Furthermore, Starov (who, again, is further discussed below) is the name of the doctor who telegrams V, the narrator-biographer, with news of Sebastian Knight's fatal illness (*RLSK* 160). The 'Icarus', a supposed sports car favoured in more than one early Nabokov novel, takes a return spin. Intimations of, or nods toward, a number of further Nabokov works ('The Return of Chorb', 'The Vane Sisters', *The Eye*, and others) can be spotted by the more sleuthful reader.

There is a further range of references (or near-references) deriving rather from Nabokov's own biography than from his fiction. The tie-up between 'you' and Véra has already been briefly treated, while Boyd points out that 'Vadim's first three wives are all constructed as virtual color negatives of Véra' (*B Am* 632). The 'Mr V.S.' with whom the London specialist allegedly confuses Vadim (*LATH* 18) is presumably V. Sirin, pen-name in Russian émigré letters of Nabokov; Vadim himself used the pen name 'V. Irisin' (deriving from his first wife, Iris: see *LATH* 82). Therefore 'Vadim Vadimovich' is to Vladimir Vladimirovich, as 'V. Irisin' is to V. Sirin. Vadim seems occasionally to be called 'Vivian' (*LATH* 41, 194), thus conjuring up shades of 'Vivian Darkbloom', and other anagrammatic Nabokovian appellations. In Leningrad Vadim feels there is something familiar about 'the façade of a house on Gertsen [Herzen] Street' (*LATH* 166), the location of the Nabokovs' St Petersburg residence. The American literary figure Gerard Adamson (*LATH* 126) would seem to suggest Edmund Wilson in that character, and he is claimed as such by Proffer (*Things*, 299; Proffer also suggests that Louise, consequently, is Mary McCarthy).

It is frequently said that Vadim is to be seen as a kind of anti-Nabokov, and indeed, he has many features and actions seemingly diametrically opposite to those of his better half: active nymphetry and other indiscretions in the disclosure of his sexual autobiography; his attitude to (and details concerning) childhood, parents, and princely title; the act of killing a border guard while fleeing Soviet Russia (although one might compare this with an incident in Crimea in which a 'bow-legged Bolshevik sentry attempted to arrest [Nabokov] for signaling (with my net, he said) to a British warship': *SM* 103); a declared lack of interest in lepidoptery and botany, as well as sports (although some details in his prose would seem to belie these prejudices); his apparent unpopularity as a lecturer; and the discomfiting vagueness over time and memory. On the other hand, he does share certain Nabokovian traits (beyond a general literary and biographical profile): a dislike of Dostoevsky, Freud, Marx, and modern art; and several shared working practices. Moreover, for all his supposed inferiority to his original, or unnamed and unseen double, it seems that Vadim, like Nabokov himself, is spoken of as a likely Nobel laureate.

By now it goes without saying that wordplay is Nabokov's stock-in-trade. Much of this in *LATH* is, as we have seen, self-referential on various levels – 'nastily hermetic' is a 'compliment' said to be paid to Vadim's prose by one critic (*LATH* 85). However, *LATH* also has a structured system of wordplay of its own, and this has been admirably explicated by Johnson in his *Worlds in Regression* (and updated and summarized in *GCVN* 330–40). This centres on the theme of incest, itself, of course, reprised from earlier works, and the persona, and name, of Count Nikifor Nikodimovich Starov, Vadim's 'benefactor' and 'a grave old-fashioned Mason who had graced several great Embassies during a gracious span of international intercourse' (*LATH* 15). The admirer of Vadim's mother, Starov, 'sported some English blood' and was probably Vadim's 'real father' (*LATH* 178–9), as well as the father of Lieutenant Wladimir Blagidze, alias Starov, the ex-lover and then murderer of Vadim's first wife, Iris. Johnson adduces that Count Starov's 'international intercourse' extended to the fathering of several more characters: Iris and Ivor Black, Annette, and possibly even Vadim's third wife, Louise. The clues to this are the 'star' quality from the Count's name and the 'bl' consonantal combination in other key names (Black, Blagidze, and Blagovo, Annette's maiden name), and certain opaquely expressed circumstances in the relevant backgrounds. As Johnson points out, Nabokov professed a fondness for the 'bl' sound 'in siblings, bloom, blue, bliss, sable' (*SO* 123), rather than any obsession with incest as such, and the name Starover Blue (a professor of astronomy) occurs in *Pale Fire* (*PF* 186–7). If Dr Starov was an angel of death in *The Real Life of Sebastian Knight*, then Count Starov seems in *LATH* to have been a demon of birth. Certainly, if we accept Johnson's analysis, incestuous relations abound in Nabokov's last novel, as they did in *Ada*.

Once such significance has been attached to star/Starov, an extensive stellar leitmotif can be readily recognized, and the textual evidence adduced by Johnson augmented. On 'the fourth or fifth anniversary' of Iris's death, Vadim 'sobs as he walks' through the streets of Paris, moved by a couplet of Russian verse 'that he hideously mistakes for his own', translated as: 'Heavenly stars are seen as stellate only through tears' (*LATH* 76; a more literal version might read: 'the star-shapedness of the heavenly stars you see only through tears'). Following this, the bookseller Oksman's references to what sound like the books and the father of the real Vladimir

Nabokov remind Vadim of his 'especial dread that I might be permanently impersonating somebody living as a real being beyond the constellation of my tears and asterisks' (*LATH* 82). Decades later, when Vadim and Louise have seen Bel for the last time, Vadim observes: 'The aquamarine sky was now silent, darkish and empty, save for a star-shaped star about which I wrote a Russian elegy ages ago, in another world' (*LATH* 155). Problems of identity and authorship here apart, the star motif apparently connects Vadim with Iris, Louise, and Bel. Some years earlier, in America, Vadim had been disconcerted by 'the moist starry stare' of his estranged second wife Annette, as he mistakes for Bel a child she is minding (*LATH* 127).

Bel's connection with the Starov constellation is necessarily at a remove, but her poem, read to Vadim, repeats Iris's reference to a dead dog ('*Dors, Médor!*': *LATH* 39) in the line '*Médor, a dead dog*'; decades later again, Vadim, on rereading these lines, can 'see through their starry crystal' the possibility of writing a 'tremendous commentary... with galaxies of reference marks' (136–7). *See under Real*, Vadim's first attempt at a fictionalized biography in English, descends under manically indignant editing by the dead novelist's brother into a mass of 'astronomical symbols bespeckling the text' (as though Kinbote has taken up Sebastian Knight); not surprisingly, perhaps, this book never gets beyond 'its hard-cover instar' (*LATH* 101).

Louise's connection seems even more tenuous, through the good offices of her ' "English" cousin', Lady Fay Morgain (*fata Morgana, Morgain la fée*, or Morgan le Fay); this Fay came from a diplomatic background and was aquainted with 'little Iris Black in London, around 1919', when she herself had been 'a starry-eyed American gal' (*LATH* 139–41). Even 'you' might just conceivably be connected to the Starov dynasty: 'in principle', according to Johnson, her father might have been the critic Demian Basilevski (he who had found Vadim's fiction 'nastily hermetic' – note, too, the displaced 'bl' in his name – and later seeming to run a critical journal in Russian New York, where 'you' has family ties: *LATH* 105, 179).[12] Just before Vadim's near-fatal collapse, however, he mentally visualizes 'you' reading the index cards comprising *Ardis*:

> I caressed the facets of the Blackwing pencil you kept gently twirling, I felt against my raised knees the fifty-year-old folded

chessboard, Nikifor Starov's gift (most of the noblemen were badly chipped in their baize-lined mahogany box!), propped on your skirt with its pattern of irises. My eyes moved with yours, my pencil queried with your own faint little cross in the narrow margin a solecism I could not distinguish through the tears of space. (*LATH* 183)

'You' is here, in some literary and biographical pattern within Vadim's exploding consciousness, linked with 'Black', Starov, defective noblemen, 'Iris', 'a faint cross', and 'tears'. Johnson has suggested an anagrammatic significance to the phrase 'the constellation of my *tears* and *asterisks*' (his emphasis: *GCVN* 339), betokening what he calls 'the phantasmagoric familial galaxy of Count Starov'. 'Tears' does, of course, contain the word 'star', but it is also an anagram of 'stare', and 'Stare at the Asterisks!' would have made another fitting alternative title for *LATH*.

Not just 'one of the characters', Dementia or 'incipient lunacy' (*LATH* 179) takes on the role, Johnson stresses, of 'leading lady, at least until she is displaced by "Reality" in the form of VV's last love' (*GCVN* 332). Vadim's mental condition is really one of schizophrenia, or split identity (see Johnson, *GCVN* 335–9), connected to or thereby explaining his left–right obsession. The 'Reality' that enters upon his recovery at the end of the book (*LATH* 195) represents both the person of his ideal love and the reintegration of his long-divided self. This has been immediately preceded by the struggle to regain identity (*LATH* 193–4). VV knows that he is 'Vadim Vadimovich', surname beginning with 'N' and containing a 'B': he tries out 'Nebesnyy', 'Nabedrin', 'Nablidze', 'Naborcroft', 'Blonsky', and is puzzled by 'allusions to a Mr Nabarro'.[13] Only when he had given up his 'sonorous surname crept up from behind, like a prankish child'.

'Vadim Vadimych', in its colloquial form, is barely distinguishable from a slurred colloquial pronunciation of 'Vladimir Vladimirovich', he realizes. The unseen 'original' author, of course, has to be Nabokov; however, this is not the *real* Nabokov (who did not in all seriousness consistently hallucinate an alternative biography for himself), but a projected 'Vladimir Vladimirovich' persona, who remains but a shadow. Upon

111

returning to 'reality' (the term being, as ever, relative), this author writes the demented autobiography of his alternative, or 'left-sided' personality (and hence his previous left–right/insane–sane obsession). The demented origins of this narrative thus also account for its highly improbable patterning (the Starov incest complex and the 'bl' cluster).

'Poor Vivian, poor Vadim Vadimovich, was but a figment of somebody's – not even my own – imagination', avers the primary narrator (as he now appears); musing on the near-sonic equivalence of 'Vladimir Vladimirovich' and 'Vadim Vadimovich', he cites the example of '"Pavel Pavlovich", Paul, son of Paul' sounding as 'Pahlpahlych' (*LATH* 194). A certain 'Pahl Pahlich' (ex-husband of Nina Lecerf, presumed to be Sebastian's last love) thus styles himself in *The Real Life of Sebastian Knight*, in the company of a chess-playing cousin, dubbed 'Black' (*RLSK* 118).[14] In like fashion, and perhaps more significantly as an evocation, Pnin introduces himself to his (roughly speaking) stepson Victor as '"Timofey Pavlovich Pnin", which means "Timothy the Son of Paul"', or colloquially, 'Timofey Pahlch' (*P* 86). *Pnin*, too, has a Nabokovian persona as primary narrator. An exemplary model for this device is Pushkin's *Eugene Onegin*, and Maddox has drawn attention to the *Onegin* allusions in *LATH*, centring on Vadim's visit to Leningrad.[15] However, there is also a further possible Pushkin link: Vadim's supposedly official father, as he claims, 'died in a pistol duel with a young Frenchman' (*LATH* 82). Pushkin, in a different time and place, had been fatally wounded duelling with the Frenchman d'Anthès; Vadim would therefore seem to be considering himself, at another level, as a son of Pushkin.

Dementia and identity anxiety form one side of VV's condition, impelling him into 'the endless re-creation of my fluid self' through the writing of fiction (*LATH* 82); time and space are another. Notes on 'the Substance of Space', or 'tussles with the Specter of Space' (*LATH* 175, 181), in connection with Vadim's novel *Ardis*, clearly correspond to Van Veen's 'The Texture of Time'. Only at the end of the novel is Vadim (or the erstwhile Vadim), in the words of 'you', 'a sane man who could tell the difference between time and space' (*LATH* 196). Back in his Quirn days[16] he had made a plainly premature attempt to write

'*The Invisible Lath*, a book rather similar to that in the reader's hands' (*LATH* 123). The left/right disorientation is connected in Vadim's mind with mirrors, as well as with space and time ('rolling the world round on its axis' or 'travelling back physically from the present moment to the previous one': *LATH* 185). The reverse mirror image (gazing at his naked self in a mirror, plus the appearance of a butterfly and the confession of the left/right condition, constitute his pre-proposal ritual to prospective wives) corresponds to the inverted fictional world created by Vadim in *LATH*. Johnson links this to the two-world cosmology described in Martin Gardner's *The Ambidextrous Universe*, a work of popular science known to have interested Nabokov:[17] VV and Vladimir Vladimirovich may even be existing, it is suggested, in different dimensions, while the whole may be seen as a variation on the two-world theme as expressed through many of Nabokov's works.

From such an analysis there emerges the following authorial/narratorial hierarchy: Nabokov himself (as historical author, and as implied author of this novel); 'Vladimir Vladimirovich', as projected authorial persona, or unseen narrator; and Vadim Vadimovich, the unseen narrator's demented *alter ego*. Putting the same scheme in terms of worlds would give a similar hierarchy, descending from the real historical world of Vladimir Nabokov, through the fictionalized world of the 'Vladimir Vladimirovich' persona, and indeed the fictional worlds created in the literary works of Nabokov/'Vladimir Vladimirovich' (in this sense, probably inseparable), to what purports – in the fiction – to be the 'real' world of the putative author Vadim Vadimovich (or, at least, his perceptions of it), down, finally, to the fictional worlds (at these several removes) allegedly created by him.

But we can perhaps go further in our interrogation of time in *LATH*. 'Nobody can imagine in physical terms the act of reversing the order of time. Time is not reversible', declares 'you' on the final page of the book. The now 'cured' Vadim (transported to 'Catapult, California') finds her explanation of his problem, 'his morbid mistake', as having 'confused direction and duration', to be 'merely an exquisite quibble'; nevertheless, he contends that 'the notion of trying to twirl time is a *trouvaille*' (*LATH* 197). This 'find' seems reminiscent of the 'rechewing' and 'rebelching' process envisaged at the end of *The Gift*; Fyodor has earlier said, 'I seem to remember my future works' (*G* 179), and we may also recall Nabokov's lines of 1919 on the 'The far-off crests of future works . . . / . . . concealed / like mountaintops in pre-auroral mist' (*PP* 23). Could there be, inbuilt in the system of *LATH*, something of what Gardner would call 'a twist in the grain of space–time'?[18] There are at least three pointers within the text that could lend support to such a 'time twirling', or Möbius-strip-like, interpretation.

Firstly, let us turn briefly again to Vadim's four wives. Without disputing Boyd's view of the first three as 'virtual color negatives of Véra' and of 'you', indeed, as the latter (*B Am* 632; 'she *is* Véra', 633), there is still a sense in which the four constitute a continuum, with variations on the required qualities (background, appearance, sexuality, fidelity; linguistic and secretarial capabilities; intellect, erudition, and Muse potential), culminating in the ideal – 'you'. Iris, said to be 21 at the time of the first Carnavaux summer (*LATH* 17), would be almost exactly the age of Véra (born 5 January 1902). All four are treated to the same bizarre proposal routine. 'You' is born on the same day as daughter Bel, with the two recollected together as 'looking like twins', while ' "*Metamorphoza*", you said in your lovely, elegant Russian' (*LATH* 177). As Johnson has suggested, Bel's twinning with 'you' corresponds to those of Vadim Vadimovich with 'Vladimir Vladimirovich' and 'V. Irisin' with V. Sirin.[19] In the dualized existence of the writer (VV/'Vladimir Vladimirovich'), 'you', walking through the door, now as 'Reality', could be either (or indeed both) the age 'you'/Bel is meant to be (28) at the time of Vadim's collapse (1970), or (if 'she *is* Véra') the then age of Véra herself.

And what of Vadim himself? On the verge of falling in love with his prospective second wife, Annette, in the context of a wet dream with 'a somewhat infantile setting, marked by exquisite aching stirrings that I knew as a boy, as a youth, as a madman, as an old dying voluptuary' (and we may note the four ages of man, here corresponding to four wives), Vadim throws in the curious remark: 'my average age has been thirteen all my life' (*LATH* 86, 87). While this may seem a self-deprecating recognition of an arrested adolescent attitude to sexuality, in full accordance with a lasting penchant for nymphets, mathematically it implies a final age of 26. Thus, at some level at least, Vadim may still be in his twenties, close to the age of 'you' and to that of Fyodor at the end of *The Gift* (these ages may not relate exactly to any form of actuality, but everything is somewhat skewed in *LATH*). Vadim/ 'Vladimir Vladimirovich' may therefore be simultaneously at the beginning of his literary career, anticipating through a mist 'the far-off crests of future works', and at the end of it (or imagining himself at the end of it) looking back, catapulted from a state of near death by process of dream, metamorphosis, and the twirling of time.

Conversely there may also be found in the earlier part of *LATH* a possible version of Vadim (and of 'you') at an advanced age. On the Riviera beach with Iris, Vadim enquires of her 'the nationality of the bronzed old man with the hoary chest hair who was wading out of the low surf preceded by his dog – I thought I knew his face'; this question is not answered, but he is said to be 'Kanner, the great pianist and butterfly hunter' (*LATH* 29–30). Presently, descending to the beach, Vadim hears 'a roar of unearthly ecstasy'; 'I do hope it's not a happy escapee from Kanner's Circus', says Iris. 'No relation – at least, so it seemed – to the pianist', adds the narrator (*LATH* 33). The explanation lies in a butterfly net, as old Kanner appears, 'his white locks flying around his scarlet brow, and the whole of his person still radiating ecstasy'; the apparently Germanic Kanner refers to '*eine* "Pandora"...a common southern *Falter* (butterfly)' (*LATH* 34). The 'Paon d'Or' ('or "Pandora"') turns up later as the restaurant in which Vadim dines with Iris and Ivor before Iris's murder,[20] while Falter is, of course, also the name of the demented visionary from the story 'Ultima Thule'. We may also recall Nabokov's triumphant shriek of lepidopteral capture in childhood (*SM* 106) and the double-identity trick of the Crimean playlet 'In Spring'. On the beach, we are told: '[t]he pianist's dog was today in the company of a handsome old lady, his fourth wife' (*LATH* 35). Kanner's white locks are matched by the 'leonine locks' of the older Vadim, 'done away with' by a 'thorough haircut' (*LATH* 178).

Nabokov (sometimes accompanied by his wife) frequently makes fleeting appearances in his works, often identified through the occupation of lepidoptery. But why should he be Germanic? One striking difference between Vadim's biography and that of Nabokov is the absence of a period of residence in Germany. Kanner seems therefore to represent a Nabokovian projection of an exaggerated Germanic period in his own career totally missing in that of Vadim. The name 'Kanner' is a slight extension of the German word *Kanne*, a jug, and a synonym of *Krug* (but meaning 'circle' in Russian). 'Krug' suggests Adam Krug, the protagonist of *Bend Sinister*, himself a Nabokovian projection catapulted (though eventually 'saved' by his creator at the point of death) into a nightmare anti-Utopian world; Krug is a philosopher, Kanner a pianist. His dog recalls the twice-mentioned 'Médor' as well as sundry curs sprinkled through Nabokov's works. Kanner may also be reminiscent of Udo Conrad, a German writer resident in France in *Laughter in the Dark*, also taken as a Nabokovian representative. As a lepidopterist, Kanner carries a butterfly net, the lack of which in the Rocky Mountains gives Vadim 'the dream sensation of having come empty-handed – without what? A gun? A wand?' (*LATH* 123), while Vadim had earlier contemplated transforming himself into 'say, a lepidopterist' (82).

The butterfly net or wand, of course, is here the Harlequin's wooden sword or lath, 'the omnipresent symbol of the autobiography's title motif' (Johnson, *GCVN*, 337). In *The Gift* each of Fyodor's poems 'iridesces with harlequin colours' (*G* 32). Decades later in *LATH*, Kanner, who is seemingly – and aptly – also in some sense a circus master, appears as the final Hitchcockian self-representation, a burlesque of the ultimate Harlequin in full maturity: Vladimir Nabokov.

LATH is not normally counted as one of Nabokov's most successful novels. As already indicated, it is arguably the least accessible to all but the Nabokov connoisseur. As a literary performance it is often held to be uneven. 'Perhaps the motley failures of style are *all* deliberate, the patches of Vadim's harlequin self,' suggests Boyd (*B Am* 625). Nevertheless, *LATH* demands, and indeed repays, full critical attention as a fittingly culminating work, amounting to a comprehensive retrospective on an astonishing lifetime of literary achievement.

Notes

For full details of the works quoted below, see Bibliography. For abbreviated works, see previously listed Abbreviations and References.

PREFACE

1 Edmund White, 'Nabokov: Beyond Parody', in Gibian and Parker (1984), 5–27, at p. 18.
2 Ibid., 19, 23.
3 Frank Kermode, *History and Value: The Clarendon Lectures and the Northcliffe Lectures 1987* (Oxford: Clarendon Press, 1988), 16.
4 Lodge (1997), 152.
5 White, pp. 12, 18.
6 Adams (1992), 3.
7 White, p. 11.

CHAPTER 1. INTRODUCTION: A VN SURVEY

1 *Sirin*, a mythological Russian bird, had also been the name of an important publishing imprint in pre-revolutionary Russia, specializing in Symbolist works, including Bely's *Petersburg* (1913).
2 The sprinkling of German words and expressions in his works, family background (V. D. Nabokov certainly knew German) and boyhood visits apart, it seems barely credible that Nabokov could have spent fifteen years in a European country without acquiring some of the language. A revealing 'slip', moreover, might be the comment in *Nikolai Gogol* (1944) contrasting a detail of Russian with 'the other three European languages I happen to know' (*NG* 63): these could only have been English, French, and German.
3 Brian Boyd, however, suggests that very little of this work had been written down by the time of Nabokov's death (*B Am* 642, 658–9).
4 In later years Nabokov cultivated a very definite persona; as Boyd puts it, '"V.N." was a game he played to the hilt' (*B Rus* 309–10).

5 Beaujour (1989), 81–117, gives a convincing account of Nabokov's bilingual 'trajectory' (at pp. 88, 89, 92).

6 Ibid. 108.

7 The leading commentators on these twin approaches to Nabokov's metaphysics are Alexandrov (*Nabokov's Otherworld*, 1991) and Johnson (*Worlds in Regression*, 1985: see particularly Chapter 6, 'Nabokov as Gnostic Seeker'). See also Boyd (1985) and the critical sections of *B Rus* and *B Am*.

8 Alexandrov (1991), 55.

9 Ibid. 3, 88, 98. On metafiction, as the self-conscious laying bare of fiction as device, see Hutcheon (1984) and Waugh (1984).

10 See Foster (1993) on Nabokov and modernism; on late and post-modernism, see McHale (1987 and 1992).

11 Ibid. 6. The spectrum of otherworldly practice in Nabokov criticism ranges from the sophisticatedly insightful (as in the case of Alexandrov) to the crudely vulgar (who shall here be nameless).

12 Some examples of early Russian criticism are included in the collections edited by Appel and Newman (1970) and Page (1982); the first monographs are those by Stegner (1966) and Field (1967).

13 Notably those by Grabes (1977), Grayson (1977), and Hyde (1977), plus collections of essays or special issues of journals.

14 In the first category, see Pifer (1980), Rampton (1984), and Toker (1989), and the essay by Rorty (1989); in the second, see Boyd (1985), Meyer (1988), and Barabtarlo (1989); the most notable books in the third category are Johnson (1985) and Tammi (1985).

15 See, for instance, Connolly (1992) and Foster (1993); an important anthology of criticism published in Russian is *V. V. Nabokov: Pro et Contra* (1997); essays by some Russian critics are beginning to appear also in English (as are writings by leading American-based Russian commentators, such as Sergei Davydov and Aleksandr Dolinin: see Bibliography).

16 On *Despair*, see Cornwell (1998); on *Invitation to a Beheading* see, for instance, Connolly (1997) and Lachmann (1997).

CHAPTER 2.   VN: THE CRITIC

1 On Nabokov and Joyce, see Cornwell (1992), 71–9; and Julian Moynahan in *GCVN*, 433–44. On the complexities of Nabokov, Joyce, and modernism, see Foster (1993), *passim*.

2 See Terence Killeen, 'Nabokov... Léon... Joyce', *The Irish Times* (June 13, 1992), 8; and Neil Cornwell, 'More on Joyce and Russia: Or *Ulysses* on the Moscow River', *Joyce Studies Annual 1994* (Austin: University of Texas Press, 1994), 175–86, at p. 176.

3 A seventh printing of Martin Parker's translation of Mikhail Lermontov, *A Hero of Our Time*, appeared in 1985 (Moscow: Raduga); the first printings date from 1947 and 1951 under the Foreign Languages Publishing House imprint (subsequently Progress and eventually Raduga); a revised edition, edited by the present author, was published under the Everyman imprint (London: J. M. Dent, 1995). On the Nabokov translation see William Mills Todd III, in *GCVN*, 178–83.

4 See Brian Boyd's analysis (*B Am* 318–55) and that by Alexander Dolinin in *GCVN*, 117–30.

CHAPTER 3.   VN: GRAND MASTER OF THE SHORT STORY

1 On Nabokov's short stories, see in particular Naumann (1978), Nicol and Barabtarlo (1993), and the articles in *GCVN* on 'English Short Stories' (by Gennadi Barabtarlo, 101–17) and 'Russian Short Stories' (by Nataliia Tolstaia and Mikhail Meilakh, 644–60).

2 Larry R. Andrews, 'Deciphering "Signs and Symbols"', in *5th Arc*, 139–52, at p. 148.

3 William Carroll, 'Nabokov's Signs and Symbols', in *Things*, 203–17, at p. 211.

4 Field (1967), 308, and most subsequent commentators make this point.

5 See Connolly (1992), 19.

6 This story has attracted considerable critical comment: see, for example, Zholkovsky (1994), 109–13; plus Barbara Heldt Monter, '"Spring in Fialta": The Choice that Mimics Chance', in Appel and Newman (1970), 128–35; Saputelli (1986); Charles Nicol, '"Ghastly Rich Glass": A Double Essay on "Spring in Fialta"', in *RLT* 24, 173–84; Stephen Matterson, 'Sprung from the Music Box of Memory: "Spring in Fialta"', in Nicol and Barabtarlo (1993), 99–109; Foster (1993), 131–46.

7 See the Ronens (1981), 382–3.

8 Nicol describes this phenomenon in his article (cited above) in *RLT* 24.

9 See Priscilla Meyer, 'The German Theme in Nabokov's Work of the 1920s', in Nicol and Barabtarlo (1993), 3–14; Dale E. Peterson, 'Nabokov and Poe', in *GCVN*, 463–72; and Shrayer, 1997b.

CHAPTER 4.   VN: THE RUSSIAN NOVELIST: *MARY* TO *THE GIFT*

1 On this point see Toker (1989), 43–4; Connolly (1992), 232–3; and Dieter E. Zimmer, '*Mary*', in *GCVN*, 346–58.

2 On Nabokov and this period of Russian culture, see Olga Skonechanaia, '"People of the Moonlight": Silver Age Parodies in Nabokov's *The Eye* and *The Gift*', *NS*, 3 (1996), 33–52; and Alexandrov (1991), 'Conclusion', 213–34; see also Anna Brodsky, 'Homosexuality and the Aesthetic of Nabokov's *Dar*', *NS*, 4 (1987), 95–115 [publ. 1998]. On a more general 'literary' level, see Anat Ben-Amos, 'The Role of Literature in *The Gift*', ibid. 117–49.

3 Allan (1994), 68.

4 Karlinsky (1963), 285.

5 On Nabokov as self-translator, see Grayson (1977).

6 In point of fact, Nabokov based his transliteration system on the old Russian orthography, which he continued to use in his Russian writings of this period (the new orthography having been introduced by the Bolsheviks in 1918).

7 Noted by Hyde (1977), 32. On Chernyshevsky in *The Gift*, see Hyde (1977), 17–37; Rampton (1984), 64–100; Davydov (1985); and Paperno (1992); on Chernyshevsky himself, the standard study is Irina Paperno, *Chernyshevsky and the Age of Realism* (Stanford: Stanford University Press, 1988).

8 See Tammi (1985), 80–97, Toker (1989), 142–76, Alexander Dolinin, '*The Gift*' in *GCVN*, 135–69, at pp. 161–5.

9 However, Tammi (1985), 98–101, takes a contrary view on this point.

10 Karlinsky (1963), 285–6.

11 Connolly (1992), 198.

12 On keys, see Johnson (1985), 93–111; Waite (1995).

13 On the varied nuances of the 'gift', see Hyde (1977), 27; Johnson (1985), 93–4; Dolinin in *GCVN*, 142 and 166, n. 29.

14 On 'Pushkin's trace' in *The Gift* see Greenleaf (1994).

15 On urban modernist perambulation see Peter I. Barta, *Bely, Joyce, and Döblin: Peripatetics in the City Novel* (Gainesville: University Press of Florida, 1996); Foster (1993), 146–55, discusses 'covert modernism' in *The Gift*.

16 See Toker (1989), 160–2.

17 See Dolinin in *GCVN*, cited above.

18 Connolly (1992), 208–9. One critic, Long (1984), reads into *The Gift* an undermining of all the work's main features (Fyodor and his poetry, the Chernyshevski biography, the heroic father, and the love story), as 'complex layerings of irony and unaccented juxtapositions do their work of clarification' (89–100, at p. 100).

19 With regard to closure in *The Gift*, though, it should be noted that Nabokov, for a while, planned a second volume to his Russian *magnum opus* (see Boyd, *B Rus* 505–6; 516–17).

CHAPTER 5. THE *LOLITA* PHENOMENON

1 Barbara Eckstein, 'Unsquaring the Square of *What Maisie Knew*', in *The Turn of the Screw* and *What Maisie Knew*, ed. Neil Cornwell and Maggie Malone (Basingstoke and London: Macmillan, 'New Casebooks', 1998), 179–93, writes: '*Lolita* is surely a burlesque of *What Maisie Knew* and also an exercise in slippery self-parody', at p. 190. On Nabokov and James, see Gregory (1984).

2 Rayfield (1984), 74.

3 Ibid. 141.

4 Nabokov, *Sobranie sochinenii* (Moscow, 1990), 4, 250; see also Rayfield (1984), 140. Dolinin (1993) adds a story by a minor émigré writer named Valentin Samsonov as another possible source; see also Ernest Machen's letter in *TLS* (November 27 1998), 17. See also Julian Connolly, 'Nabokov's Dialogue with Dostoevsky: *Lolita* and "The Gentle Creature"', in *NS*, 4 (1997), 15–36 [publ. 1998], for comparisons with that story.

5 See Olsen (1995), 16–25, for one recent account. On reactions at Cornell to *Lolita*, see Diment (1997) *passim* (but especially pp. 60–8 and 141–6).

6 See Appel's notes to *The Annotated Lolita* (*L*). Proffer (1968), 21–3, lists over 60 names. Further notes have been supplied by Brian Boyd in *Novels 1955–1962* (1996), 873–91.

7 See Meyer (1988), 13–38, on Pushkin (*Lolita* and *Onegin*); other Russian writers (including Tolstoy and Lermontov) may also be discerned; the use made of numbers may derive from Pushkin (*The Queen of Spades*), and the attention to names from Gogol.

8 Fredric Jameson, *The Seeds of Time* (New York: Columbia University Press, 1994), 147; Lorna Sage, *Angela Carter* (Plymouth: Northcote House, 1994), 29. Linda Kauffman's essay, 'Framing Lolita: Is There a Woman in the Text?' (a rare feminist reading of *Lolita*), in Bloom (1993), 149–68, discusses Lolita as both consumer and consumed.

9 Olsen (1995), 44; on 'comic romance' see Long (1984) 135–51.

10 Trevor McNeely, '"Lo" and Behold: Solving the *Lolita* Riddle', in Bloom (1993), 134–48, at p. 143.

11 Amis (1992), 109. See also Sarah Herbold, 'Reflections on Modernism: *Lolita* and Political Engagement, or How the Left and the Right Both Have it Wrong', in *NS*, 3 (1996), 145–50, on the dilemma posed between 'law and narrative desire'.

12 Richard H. Bullock 'Humbert the Character, Humbert the Writer', in Bloom (1993), 90–104.

13 Identified in Bruss (1976); developed by Christina Tekiner, 'Time in *Lolita*', *Modern Fiction Studies*, 25 (1979), 463–9; discussed further by

Toker (1989), 209–11.

14 See Alexander Dolinin, 'Nabokov's Time Doubling: from *The Gift* to *Lolita*', *NS*, 2 (1995), 3–40; and Julian W. Connolly, '"Nature's Reality" or Humbert's "Fancy"?: Scenes of Reunion and Murder in *Lolita*', in ibid. 41–61. The counter-case is put by Brian Boyd, '"Even Homais Nods": Nabokov's Fallibility, or, How to Revise *Lolita*', in ibid. 62–86.

15 This possibility has been raised by Proffer (1968), 82; Bullock, in Bloom (1993), 101; and Connolly, '"Nature's Reality"', 44.

16 Dolinin, Nabokov's Time Doubling', 22 and 34.

17 On this point see Tammi (1985), 281.

18 'Postscript to the Russian Edition of *Lolita*', translated by Earl D. Sampson, in *5th Arc*, 188–94.

19 See Barabtarlo (1993), 115. As it is, some editions published in Russia have appeared without the John Ray 'Foreword': for example, the 'supplementary' vol. 5 (to the *Sobranie sochinenii* in 4 vols., Moscow 1990), under the imprint Ekopros (1992).

20 See Barabtarlo (1993), 115, and Alexander Dolinin, '*Lolita* in Russian', in *GCVN*, 321–30.

21 See Corliss (1994), 47, 52; Baxter (1997), 153–9.

22 However, Corliss (1994), 86, has noted an apparent discrepancy in the repeat of Scene 1 at the end: 'this time, something is missing: the liquor bottle that had teetered on Quilty's head and, with its crashing, announced his presence. The villain, it seems, has vanished. And Humbert has walked into a parallel nightmare, where his righteous revenge may never be satisfied'.

23 Kael (1994), 205.

24 Corliss (1994), 86–7.

25 Linda Holt, 'Pornograpples', *TLS* (May 29 1998), 23.

CHAPTER 6. 'PALE FIRE'/*PALE FIRE*

1 Adams (1977), 151; Robert Merrill, 'Nabokov and Fictional Artifice', *Modern Fiction Studies*, 25 (1979), 439–62, at p. 459; Torgovnick (1986), 25.

2 See Genette (1997).

3 For readings of Shade's poetic magnum opus *qua* poem, see in particular Field (1967), 106–13; Fowler (1974; 1982 edition), 103–12; and Wood (1994), 188–98.

4 Genette (1977), 343.

5 See Johnson (1985), 68–73, for the fullest exposition of the Kinbote–Botkin question. See also *B Am* 709, n. 4, for Nabokov's diary confirmation of what in the event was calculable from the text: 'the

nasty commentator is not an ex-king and not even Dr. Kinbote, but Prof. Vseslav Botkin, a Russian and a madman'. On the historical figure of V. P. Botkin, see Meyer (1988), 115–17.

6 Torgovnick (1986), 28, here extends Bloomian 'anxiety of influence' into Kinbotean critical activity.

7 Johnson (1985), 67–8; see also objections raised by Lodge (1997), 162–4. Boyd, previously an advocate of the 'Shade as total author' theory (see *B Am* 425–56) has now modified his position to one in which the shade of Shade posthumously helps to inspire Kinbote's 'apparatus': see his 'Shade and Shape in *Pale Fire*', in *Nabokov Studies*, 4 (1997), 173–224 [published 1998], and his forthcoming book, *Nabokov's 'Pale Fire': The Magic of Artistic Discovery*. Long (1984), 178, making no reference at all to Botkin, sees Kinbote and Shade as an archetypal 'strange central pair'.

8 Pekka Tammi, '*Pale Fire*', in *GCVN*, 571–86, at p. 583; see also Tammi (1985), 198–201, on the narrative scheme of *PF*.

9 See Grabes (1977) 55–9. *Pale Fire* has also been accorded 'A Chronology' by Kevin Pilon, and 'Preliminary Annotation' to Kinbote's Commentary, by Alden Sprowles (*Things*, 218–25 and 226–47), while Gerard de Vries has appended his own supplementary 'Index' as part of his article 'Fanning the Poet's Fire. Some Remarks on Nabokov's *Pale Fire*', in *RLT*, 24 (1991), 239–67 (at pp. 259–61). Brian Boyd has supplied annotation in *Novels 1955–1962* (1996), 891–903.

10 Noted by Maddox (1983), 21–2.

11 Fowler (1982), 115–16, suggests that the diatribe against 'a so-called Pink' (*PF* 209) reflects the voice of Nabokov rather than of Kinbote. Outlining the idea of *Pale Fire* in a letter of March 1957, Nabokov includes a strangely prescient reference to 'President Kennedy', who was not to be elected until 1960 (*SL* 212–13). For another bizarre historical angle, concerning incidents at the League of Nations in 1920, see Peter Steiner, 'Zembla: A Note on Nabokov's *Pale Fire*', in Brostrom (1984), 265–72.

12 Monarchy and its trappings, however, were metaphorically used by him elsewhere: see the English poem 'An Evening of Russian Poetry' (1945), which includes the line 'Beyond the seas where I have lost a sceptre', as well as 'My back is Argus-eyed. l live in danger. / False shadows turn to track me as I pass' (*Poems*, 1961, 21–2; also in *PP* 158–63).

13 Meyer (1988).

14 Laurence Sterne, *The Life and Opinions of Tristram Shandy, Gentleman* (Harmondsworth: Penguin, 1967), 205. There are, furthermore, mentions of Zembla in three works by Defoe, including *The Farther Adventures of Robinson Crusoe*. See also Hawthorne's 'The Snow-Image'.

15 For instance, the (upstate New York) poem by Charles Fenno Hoffman (1806-84), *The Ambuscade: A Tradition of Lake Iroquois, or Champlain*, includes the line 'Of the closely-woven hazel shade', as well as 'Thrid the witch-hazel and the alder-maze'. John Clare uses the phrase twice (and even has a poem entitled 'We stood beneath the hazel shade'); other English poets using it include Robert Story, Martin Farquhar Tupper, and William Sidney Walker. For further details of all these, see the Chadwyck-Healey Literature online database at http://lion.chadwyck.co.uk/frames/e_poet.

16 See Meyer and Hoffman (1997).

17 Meyer (1988), 113–14; supported by Herbert Grabes, 'Nabokov and Shakespeare: The English Works', in *GCVN*, 496–512. Other usages of the phrase 'pale fire' are to be found in John Fletcher's *The Faithful Shepherdess* of 1679 ('This pale fire will be thy friend', V. i); and in Shelley's poem 'A Vision of the Sea' (1820).

18 Fowler (1982), 97. Field (1967), 300, considers death 'the subject of *Pale Fire*'.

19 *Peter Schlemihl*, by Adelbert Chamisso [etc.] (London: Cassell and Company, 1894). This tale is also known through Hoffmann's *The Lost Reflection*, during the course of which Erasmus Spikker, who lacks his mirror image, meets the shadowless Schlemihl. The selling of a shadow as a motif is also used by Dinesen, in her story *The Dreamers*.

20 For an instructive attempt at summarizing the inter-level correlations, see Tammi (1985), 206–17.

21 Fowler (1982), 119.

22 See Foster (1993), 221–6, who finds a key source here in 'toilest' (*PF* 154), *aka* T. S. Eliot.

23 Alexandrov (1991), 201.

24 Stegner (1967 edition), 122–3.

25 See Tammi (1985), 204–6, for one summary of this.

26 Parker (1987), 100.

27 Juliana Bordereau's famous denunciation of the narrator: Henry James, *The Aspern Papers* and *The Turn of the Screw* (Harmondsworth: Penguin, 1984), 125. Not for the only time in Nabokov, one might also invoke the spirit of James's story *The Figure in the Carpet*.

28 Indeed, these two companies, Chrysler and Daimler Benz, were to merge in 1998!

29 A possible joke at the expense of émigré Russian scholars, such as Boris Unbegaun? He indeed wrote *Russian Versification* (Oxford, 1956); and subsequently (though post-*Pale Fire*) *Russian Surnames* (Oxford, 1972).

30 Wood (1994), 186 and 203, will have none of this, considering it 'authorial trespass'; see also Lodge (1997), 162, on the 'intentional fallacy'.

31 David Rampton's phrase: see Rampton (1984), 160.

CHAPTER 7.   ARDOR IN ARDIS: *ADA*

1 Boyd (1985), 211; see also Boyd's two updated endeavours to foster a readership for *Ada: B. Am* 536–62; and '*Ada*', in *GCVN* 3–18.
2 On the phenomenon of *mise en abyme* in *Ada*, see Cancogni (1985), 108–30. It is tempting to think that the Don Juan film may owe something to Alexander Korda's *The Private Life of Don Juan* (1934), starring an ageing Douglas Fairbanks in his last film.
3 Tammi (1985), 176, however, counts 42 separate segments attributable to Ada.
4 Johnson (1985), 128, supplies a revised version of this.
5 Tammi (1985), 177, counts 29 such editorial insertions.
6 They were reprinted for American readers in *5th Arc*, 242–59; for further annotation, though, see J. E. Rivers and William Walker, 'Notes to Vivian Darkbloom's Notes to *Ada*', in *5th Arc*, 260–95; Carl R. Proffer, '*Ada* as Wonderland: A Glossary of Allusions to Russian Literature', in *Things*, 249–79; Brian Boyd, 'Annotations to *Ada*', starting with '1. Part 1, Chapter 1', *The Nabokovian*, 30 (Spring 1993), 9–48; and Boyd's 'Notes' to *Ada* in *Novels 1969–1974* (1996), 786–812.
7 See, respectively, Swanson (1975) and J. E. Rivers, 'Proust, Nabokov, and *Ada*', in Roth (1984), 134–57.
8 Mason (1974), 12–13.
9 Charles Nicol, 'Ada or Disorder', in *5th Arc*, 230–41, at 232.
10 Johnson (1985), 125; Maddox (1983), 111, also made a similar suggestion.
11 Johnson (1985), 127.
12 Johnson (1985), 131–2. Rampton (1984), 130, who sees Ada's infidelity as stemming from her muse role, writes: 'her progeny will be a "family chronicle", the words she inspires, the book to be written about her'; Ada may, though, more properly be seen as co-author.
13 Tammi (1985), 172–3.
14 Identified by Mason (1974), 165.

CHAPTER 8.   LOOKING AT THE HARLEQUINS

1 Hyde (1977), 214, 219, 220 n. 4.
2 Some of these references have been identified by Carl R. Proffer, 'Things about *Look at the Harlequins!*: Some Marginal Notes', in *Things*, 295–301; and by Richard Patteson, 'Nabokov's *Look at the*

Harlequins!: Endless Recreation of the Self', *RLT* 14 (1976; published 1977), 84–98. See also Brian Boyd's 'Notes' to *LATH* in *Novels 1969–1974* (1996), 815–24.

3 Rampton (1993), 121.

4 One critic, Grabes (1977), 106, actually claims that 'he dies in the final incompleted sentence of the book'. This, at least in a literal sense, would seem a fundamental illogicality. Others seem to have ignored this line of thinking, while Maddox (1983), 173 n. 4, adjudges Grabes to have concluded this 'inexplicably'.

5 Lachmann (1997), 313. Rampton (1993), 123, terms *LATH* 'the parody of a self-parody'.

6 On the harlequin, see Grabes (1977), 120–5; Green and Swan (1993), 232–41.

7 See Boyd (1992), 28–36, for the relationship of *LATH* to masks and to Véra.

8 Maddox (1983), 147.

9 Ibid. 157–8.

10 Noted by Patteson, *RLT* 14 (1976; published 1977), 98 n. 16.

11 However, Nabokov has told us, 'On the playing fields of Cambridge, my football team used to hail me as 'Nabkov' or facetiously, 'Macnab': *Q* 121.

12 Johnson (1985), 152 n. 69; nevertheless, Johnson prefers to conclude that 'VV's final love, "you", remains outside the Starov family orbit': *GCVN* 335.

13 Glossed by Vadim himself as 'a British politician', connnected somehow with 'the London edition of *A Kingdom by the Sea* (lovely lilting title)': *LATH* 194. Sir Gerald Nabarro (1913–73) was a Conservative MP who had opposed British publication of *Lolita*. The entry on him in *Who Was Who 1971–1980* (London: Adam and Charles Black, 1981), 573, immediately precedes that on Nabokov.

14 There is also a 'Pal Palych' in the early story 'Sounds' (1923), in which the first-person narrator also addresses his mistress as 'you': *CSVN* 14–24.

15 Maddox (1983), 147–8.

16 'Quirn' probably equals Middle English *cyrnel*: kernel, or Cornell.

17 See Johnson (1985), 170–84. See also Gardner (1979 edition), 271–2, on *LATH*, which he calls 'a marvellous shorter novel'; Nabokov had used the first (1964) edition.

18 Gardner (1979), 215.

19 Johnson (1985), 179.

20 In addition to the lepidopteral connotation (*paon* is a peacock butterfly, or emperor moth), this name is almost identical to the French word *pandour*, a rapacious soldier, thus heralding the appearance of the insane Lieutenant.

Select Bibliography

At the time of writing, all seventeen of Nabokov's novels are in print in Penguin editions, together with *Speak, Memory*, four collections of his short stories, and the recent complete single-volume compilation of stories (a total of twenty-three titles). *The Enchanter*, reprinted by Picador, adds a twenty-fourth. The collection of *Selected Letters, 1940–1977* (1990), along with Brian Boyd's monumental biography in two volumes (1990–1), have also provided major contributions to the overview of Nabokov that we now have. More recent plaudits go to the compendious *The Garland Companion to Vladimir Nabokov* (edited by Vladimir E. Alexandrov, 1995), the value of which heavyweight reference work would be hard to overestimate.

It should be noted that Nabokov's Russian works (1920–40) appeared under pseudonyms: most commonly, as with the Russian novels, under the name 'V. Sirin'.

WORKS BY NABOKOV

Collections

Vozvrashchenie Chorba [The Return of Chorb] (Berlin: Slovo, 1929; repr. Ann Arbor: Ardis, 1976); title story transl. in *Details of a Sunset and Other Stories*, 1976.

Sogliadatai [The Eye – as collection] (Paris: Russkie zapiski, 1938; repr. Ann Arbor: Ardis, 1978).

Nine Stories (Norfolk, Conn.: New Directions, 1947).

Vesna v Fial'te [Spring in Fialta] (New York: Chekhov Publishing House, 1956; repr. Ann Arbor: Ardis, 1978); title story (1936) transl. in *Nabokov's Dozen* (1958).

Nabokov's Dozen: Thirteen Stories (Garden City, New York: Doubleday, 1958; London: Heinemann, 1959; Harmondsworth: Penguin, 1960).

Nabokov's Quartet, transl. by Dmitri Nabokov (New York: Phaedra, 1966; London: Weidenfeld and Nicolson, 1967).

Nabokov's Congeries, selected with a critical introduction by Page Stegner

(New York: Viking Press, 1968).

Poems and Problems [parallel text] (New York: McGraw-Hill, 1970; London: Weidenfeld and Nicolson, 1972).

A Russian Beauty and Other Stories, transl. by Dmitri Nabokov and Simon Karlinsky (New York: McGraw-Hill; London: Weidenfeld and Nicolson, 1973; Harmondsworth: Penguin, 1975).

Tyrants Destroyed and Other Stories, transl. by Dmitri Nabokov (New York: McGraw-Hill; London: Weidenfeld and Nicolson, 1975; Harmondsworth: Penguin, 1981).

Details of a Sunset and Other Stories, transl. by Dmitri Nabokov with the author (New York: McGraw-Hill; London: Weidenfeld and Nicolson, 1976; Harmondsworth: Penguin, 1994).

The Man from the USSR and Other Plays, transl. by Dmitri Nabokov (New York: Harcourt, Brace Jovanovich, 1984; San Diego: Harvest/HBJ, 1985; London: Weidenfeld and Nicolson, 1985).

Sobranie sochinenii [Collected Works], 10 vols. (Ann Arbor: Ardis, 1987–, vols., 1, 3, 6, 9, 10 published).

P'esy [Plays] (Moscow, 1990).

Romany [Novels] (Moscow, 1990).

Sobranie sochinenii [Collected Works], ed. Viktor Erofeev (4 vols.; Moscow, 1990, plus 'supplementary' vols. 5–6 (1992–5).

The Stories of Vladimir Nabokov (New York: Knopf, 1995; London: Weidenfeld and Nicolson, 1996); as *Collected Stories* (Harmondsworth: Penguin, 1997).

Novels and Memoirs 1941–1951 (New York: Library of America, 1996).

Novels 1955–1962 (New York: Library of America, 1996).

Novels 1969–1974 (New York: Library of America, 1996).

Golos skripki v pustote [A Violin's Voice in the Void: stories and poems] (Moscow, 1997).

Sobranie sochinenii amerikanskogo perioda [Collected Works of the American Period] (5 vols.; St Petersburg, 1997–).

Major Fiction

Mashen'ka (Berlin: Slovo, 1926; repr. Ann Arbor: Ardis, 1974); transl. as *Mary*, by Michael Glenny with the author (New York: McGraw-Hill, 1970; London: Weidenfeld and Nicolson, 1971; Harmondsworth: Penguin, 1973).

Korol', dama, valet (Berlin: Slovo, 1928; repr. Ann Arbor: Ardis, 1979; transl. as *King, Queen, Knave*, by Dmitri Nabokov with the author (New York: McGraw-Hill; London: Weidenfeld and Nicolson, 1968; Harmondsworth: Penguin, 1993).

Zashchita Luzhina, Sovremennye zapiski, 40–2 (1929–30); Berlin: Slovo, 1930; repr. Ann Arbor: Ardis, 1979); transl. as *The Defence*, by Michael

Scammell with the author (New York: Putnam's; London: Weidenfeld and Nicolson, 1964; Oxford: Oxford University Press, 1986); repr. as *The Luzhin Defense* (Harmondsworth: Penguin, 1994).

'Sogliadatai', *Sovremennye zapiski*, 44 (1930); transl. as *The Eye*, by Dmitri Nabokov with the author (London: Weidenfeld and Nicolson, 1966; Harmondsworth: Penguin, 1992).

Podvig, *Sovremennye zapiski*, 45–8 (1931–2); Paris: Sovremennye zapiski, 1932 (repr. Ann Arbor: Ardis, 1974); transl. as *Glory*, by Dmitri Nabokov with the author (New York: McGraw-Hill, 1971; London: Weidenfeld and Nicolson, 1972; Harmondsworth: Penguin, 1974).

Camera obskura, *Sovremennye zapiski*, 49–52 (1932–3); as *Kamera obskura*, Paris: Sovremennye zapiski, 1933 (repr. Ann Arbor: Ardis, 1978); transl. as *Camera Obscura*, by Winifred Roy (London: John Long, 1936); also as *Laughter in the Dark*, by the author (Indianapolis: Bobbs-Merrill, 1938; rev. ed. New York: New Directions, 1960; London: Weidenfeld and Nicolson, 1961; Harmondsworth: Penguin, 1963).

Otchaianie, *Sovremennye zapiski*, 54–6 (1934); Berlin: Petropolis, 1936, (repr. Ann Arbor: Ardis, 1978); transl. as *Despair*, by the author (London: John Long, 1937; rev. ed., New York: Putnam's; London: Weidenfeld and Nicolson, 1966; Harmondsworth: Penguin, 1981).

Dar', written 1933–8; *Sovremennye zapiski*, 63–7 (1937–8); 1st integral ed., New York: Izdatel'stvo imeni Chekhova, 1952; (2nd ed., Ann Arbor: Ardis, 1975); transl. as *The Gift*, by Dmitri Nabokov and Michael Scammell with the author (New York: Putnam's; London: Weidenfeld and Nicolson, 1963; Harmondsworth: Penguin, 1981).

Priglashenie na kazn', *Sovremennye zapiski*, 58–60 (1935–6); Paris: Dom Knigi, 1938; (repr. Ann Arbor: Ardis, 1979, 1984); transl. as *Invitation to a Beheading*, by Dmitri Nabokov with the author (New York: Putnam's, 1959; London: Weidenfeld and Nicolson, 1960; Harmondsworth: Penguin, 1963).

'Solus Rex' (fragment of novel), *Sovremennye zapiski*, 70 (1940); transl. as 'Solus Rex', by Dmitri Nabokov with the author, in *A Russian Beauty and Other Stories* (1973).

The Real Life of Sebastian Knight (Norfolk, Conn.: New Directions, 1941, 1959; London: Editions Poetry, 1945; London: Weidenfeld and Nicolson, 1960; Harmondsworth: Penguin, 1964).

'Ultima Thule', *Novyi zhurnal*, 1 (1942); transl. by Dmitri Nabokov with the author, in *A Russian Beauty and Other Stories* (1973).

Bend Sinister (New York: Henry Holt, 1947; London: Weidenfeld and Nicolson, 1960; Harmondsworth: Penguin, 1974).

Lolita (Paris: Olympia Press, 1955; New York: Putnam's, 1958; London: Weidenfeld and Nicolson, 1959; [Russian ed. New York: Phaedra, 1967; repr. Ann Arbor: Ardis, 1976;] Harmondsworth, Penguin, 1980; repr. 1995).

Lolita, read by Jeremy Irons (Random House Audio Publishing, 8 cassettes, 11.5 hours).

The Annotated Lolita, ed. by Alfred J. Appel, Jr. (New York: McGraw-Hill, 1971; repr. New York: Vintage, 1991; London: Weidenfeld and Nicolson, 1993; Harmondsworth: Penguin, 1995).

Pnin (Garden City, New York: Doubleday, 1957; London: Heinemann, 1957; Harmondsworth: Penguin, 1960); transl. into Russian by Gennadii Barabtarlo (Ann Arbor: Ardis, 1983).

Pale Fire (New York: Putnam's; London: Weidenfeld and Nicolson, 1962; Harmondsworth: Penguin, 1973; repr. with Introductory Essay by Mary McCarthy, 1991); transl. into Russian as *Blednyi ogon'*, by Vera Nabokova (Ann Arbor: Ardis, 1984).

Ada or Ardor. A Family Chronicle (New York: McGraw-Hill; London: Weidenfeld and Nicolson, 1969; Harmondsworth: Penguin, 1970, including 'Notes to *Ada* by Vivian Darkbloom').

Transparent Things (New York: McGraw-Hill, 1972; London: Weidenfeld and Nicolson,1973; Harmondsworth: Penguin, 1975).

Look at the Harlequins! (New York: McGraw-Hill, 1974; London: Weidenfeld and Nicolson, 1975; Harmondsworth: Penguin, 1980).

The Enchanter, transl. by Dmitri Nabokov (New York: Putnam's, 1986; London: Picador, 1987; repr. 1998); original Russian as 'Volshebnik', *RLT, 24 (1991), 9–41; Sobranie sochinenii*, 3 (Ann Arbor: Ardis, 1991).

The shorter fiction is to be found in the various collections above and complete in *The Stories of Vladimir Nabokov* (1995).

Poetry

Stikhi [Verses] (St Petersburg: privately printed, 1916).

Al'manakh. Dva puti [An Almanac. Two Paths]. With Andrei Balashov. (Petrograd: privately printed, 1918).

Grozd'. Stikhi [The Cluster. Verses] (Berlin: Gamayun, 1922; repr. Jerusalem: n.p., 1981).

Gornyi put' [The Mountain Path] (Berlin: Grani, 1923).

'Universitetskaia poema' [A University Poem], *Sovremennye zapiski*, 33 (1933), 223–54.

Stikhotvoreniia 1929–51 [Poetry, 1929–51] (Paris: Rifma, 1952).

Poems (Garden City, New York: Doubleday, 1959; London: Weidenfeld and Nicolson, 1961).

Stikhi [Verses] (Ann Arbor: Ardis, 1979).

Stikhotvoreniia i poemy [Poetry and Narrative Poems] (Moscow, 1991).

Stikhotvoreniia i poemy [Poetry and Narrative Poems] (Moscow-Kharkov, 1997).

Plays/Screenplays

'Sobytie', *Russkie zapiski*, April (1938); transl. as 'The Event', by Dmitri Nabokov, in *The Man from the USSR and Other Plays* (London: Weidenfeld and Nicolson, 1985).

'Izobretenie val'sa', *Russkie zapiski*, November (1938); transl. as *The Waltz Invention: A Play in Three Acts*, by Dmitri Nabokov (New York: Phaedra, 1966).

Lolita: A Screenplay (New York: McGraw-Hill, 1974; repr. in *Novels 1955–1962*, New York: American Library, 1996).

Memoirs and Letters

Conclusive Evidence. A Memoir (New York: Harper); as *Speak, Memory* (London: Gollancz, 1951; New York: Universal Library, 1960); rev. ed. as *Speak, Memory: An Autobiography Revisited* (New York: Putnam's; London: Weidenfeld and Nicolson, 1967; Harmondsworth: Penguin, 1969); in Russian as *Drugie berega* (New York: Izdatel'stvo imeni Chekhova, 1954; 2nd ed., Ann Arbor: Ardis, 1978).

Strong Opinions (New York: McGraw-Hill, 1973; London: Weidenfeld and Nicolson, 1974). Interviews and miscellaneous pieces.

The Nabokov–Wilson Letters 1940[–]71, ed. by Simon Karlinsky (New York: Harper and Row, 1979).

Perepiska s sestroi [Correspondence with Sister] (Ann Arbor: Ardis, 1985).

Selected Letters 1940[–]1977, ed. by Dmitri Nabokov and Matthew J. Bruccoli (New York: Harcourt Brace Jovanovich/Bruccoli Clark Layman, 1989; London: Weidenfeld and Nicolson, 1990; London: Vintage, 1991).

Literary Criticism

'Pouchkine, ou le vrai et le vraisemblable', *La Nouvelle revue française*, 25/282 (March 1937), 362–78; transl. as 'Pushkin, or the Real and the Plausible', by Dmitri Nabokov, *The New York Review of Books* (March 31, 1988), 38[–]42.

'The Lermontov Mirage', *The Russian Review*, 1/1 (1941), 31–9.

Nikolai Gogol (Norfolk, Conn.: New Directions, 1944; repr. 1961; London: Editions Poetry, 1947; Weidenfeld and Nicolson, 1973; Oxford: Oxford University Press, 1985).

Notes on Prosody (Princeton: Bollingen Foundation, 1963; London: Routledge and Kegan Paul, 1965).

Lectures on Ulysses (Bloomfield Hills, Mich. and Columbia, SC: Bruccoli Clark, 1980).

Lectures on Literature, ed. by Fredson Bowers. Intro. by John Updike (New York: Harcourt, Brace Jovanovich; London: Weidenfeld and Nicolson, 1980; London: Picador, 1983).

Lectures on Russian Literature, ed. by Fredson Bowers (New York: Harcourt, Brace Jovanovich, 1981; London: Weidenfeld and Nicolson, 1982; London: Picador, 1983).

Lectures on Don Quixote, ed. by Fredson Bowers (New York: Harcourt, Brace Jovanovich; London: Weidenfeld and Nicolson, 1983).

Translations

Nikolka Persik [Russian transl. of Romain Rolland, *Kolas Breugnon*] (Berlin: Slovo, 1922).

Ania v strane chudes [Russian transl. of Lewis Carroll, *Alice in Wonderland*] (Berlin: Gamayun, 1923; repr. New York: Dover, 1976; Ann Arbor: Ardis, 1982).

Three Russian Poets: Selections from Pushkin, Lermontov and Tyutchev (Norfolk, Conn.: New Directions, 1944); as *Pushkin, Lermontov, Tyutchev: Poems*, London: Lindsay Drummond, 1947).

A Hero of Our Time, by Mikhail Lermontov [with Dmitri Nabokov] (Garden City, New York: Doubleday, 1958; Oxford: Oxford University Press, 1984; Ardis: Ann Arbor, 1988).

The Song of Igor's Campaign: An Epic of the Twelfth Century (New York: Random House, 1960; London: Weidenfeld and Nicolson, 1961; Ardis: Ann Arbor, 1988).

Eugene Onegin, by Alexander Pushkin, 4 vols. (New York: Bollingen; London: Routledge, 1964; rev. ed., Bollingen 1975; rev. and abridged ed., 2 vols. paperback, Princeton: Princeton University Press, 1981). Translation and copious commentary.

SECONDARY SOURCES

Essays or articles to be found within publications listed below have been detailed in the 'Notes' to the main text, as and when appropriate.

Biographical and Critical Studies on Nabokov

Adams, Robert Martin, 'Vladimir Nabokov', in his *Afterjoyce: Studies in Fiction After Ulysses* (New York: Oxford University Press, 1977), 146–61.

Adams, Robert M., 'The Wizard of Lake Cayuga', *The New York Review of Books*, 39/3 (January 30, 1992), 3–5.

Alexandrov, Vladimir E., *Nabokov's Otherworld* (Princeton: Princeton University Press, 1991). Flagship study of the 'otherworld' emphasis in Nabokov criticism.

Alexandrov, Vladimir E. (ed.), *The Garland Companion to Vladimir Nabokov* (New York: Garland, 1995). An immensely valuable and compendious volume.

Allan, Nina, *Madness, Death and Disease in the Fiction of Vladimir Nabokov* (Birmingham: Birmingham Slavonic Monographs, 1994).

Alter, Robert, 'Nabokov's Game of Worlds', in his *Partial Magic: The Novel as a Self-Conscious Genre* (Berkeley: University of California Press, 1975), 180–217.

Amis, Martin, 'Lolita Reconsidered', *Atlantic* (September 1992), 109–20.

Appel, Alfred J. and Newman, Charles (eds.) *Nabokov: Criticisms, Reminiscences, Translations and Tributes, Triquarterly*, 17 (Winter 1970; and Evanston, Ill.: Northwestern University Press, 1970). An essential miscellany.

Appel, Alfred J., Jr., *Nabokov's Dark Cinema* (New York: Oxford University Press, 1974). Discusses Nabokov's debt to the cinema.

Barabtarlo, Gennady, *Phantom of Fact: A Guide to Nabokov's 'Pnin'* (Ann Arbor: Ardis, 1989).

Barabtarlo, Gennady, *Aerial View: Essays on Nabokov's Art and Metaphysics* (New York: Peter Lang, 1993).

Berdjis, Nassim Winnie, *Imagery in Vladimir Nabokov's Last Russian Novel ([Dar]), its English Translation (The Gift) and Other Prose Works of the 1930s* (Frankfurt and New York: Peter Lang, 1995).

Bloom, Harold (ed.), *Vladimir Nabokov* (New York: Chelsea House, 1987), 'Modern Critical Views'.

Bloom, Harold (ed.), *Vladimir Nabokov's 'Lolita'* (New York: Chelsea House, 1987), 'Modern Critical Interpretations'.

Bloom, Harold (ed.), *Lolita* (New York: Chelsea House, 1993), 'Major Literary Characters'. A particularly useful anthology.

Boyd, Brian, *Nabokov's 'Ada': The Place of Consciousness* (Ann Arbor: Ardis, 1985).

Boyd, Brian, *Nabokov: The Russian Years* (Princeton: Princeton University Press; London: Chatto and Windus, 1990). Definitive biography: vol. 1.

Boyd, Brian, *Nabokov: The American Years* (Princeton: Princeton University Press, 1991; London: Chatto and Windus, 1992). Definitive biography: vol. 2.

Boyd, Brian, 'The Nabokov Biography and the Nabokov Archive', *Biblion*, 1/1 (Fall 1992), 15–36.

Brown, Edward, 'Nabokov, Chernyshevsky, Olesha and the Gift of Sight', *Stanford Slavic Studies*, 4/2 (1992), 280–94.

Buks [Buhks], Nora *Eshafot v khrustal'nom dvortse: o russikh romanakh Vladimira Nabokova* (Moscow, 1998).

Cancogni, Annapaola, *The Mirage in the Mirror: Nabokov's Ada and its French Pre-texts* (New York: Garland, 1985).

Clancy, Laurie, *The Novels of Vladimir Nabokov* (London: Macmillan, 1984).

Connolly, Julian W., *Nabokov's Early Fiction: Patterns of Self and Other* (Cambridge: Cambridge University Press, 1992). A valuable study of the Russian fiction.

Connolly, Julian W. (ed.), Nabokov's *'Invitation to a Beheading'*: *A Critical Companion* (Evanston, Ill.: Northwestern University Press, 1997).

Connolly, Julian W. (ed.), *Nabokov and his Fiction: New Perspectives* (Cambridge, Cambridge University Press, 1999). A promising collection.

Corliss, Richard, *Lolita* (London: British Film Institute, 1994). The Kubrick film.

Cornwell, Neil, 'Notes on Fantastic/Gothic Elements in Nabokov's *Despair*', in *Neo-Formalist Papers: Contributions to the Silver Jubilee Conference to mark 25 years of the Neo-Formalist Circle. Held at Mansfield College, Oxford, 11–13 September 1995* (Amsterdam and Atlanta, GA: Rodopi, 1998), 168–80.

Cummins, George M., 'Nabokov's Russian *Lolita*', *Slavic and East European Journal*, 21 (1977), 354–65.

Davydov, Sergei, *'Teksty-Matreshki' Vladimira Nabokova* (Munich: Sagner, 1982).

Davydov, Sergei, '*The Gift*: Nabokov's Aesthetic Exorcism of Chernyshevskii', *Canadian-American Slavic Studies*, 19/3 (1985), 357–74.

Diment, Galya, *Pniniad: Vladimir Nabokov and Marc Szeftel* (Seattle: Washington University Press, 1997).

Dolinin, Alexander, 'Nabokov and "Third-Rate Literature" (On a Source of *Lolita*)', *Elementa*, 1 (1993), 167–73.

Field, Andrew, *Nabokov: His Life in Art* (London: Hodder and Stoughton, 1967).

Field, Andrew, *Nabokov: His Life in Part* (London: Hamish Hamilton, 1977).

Field, Andrew, *VN: The Life and Art of Vladimir Nabokov* (New York: Crown, 1986; London: Queen Anne Press, 1987).

Foster, John Burt, *Nabokov's Art of Memory and European Modernism* (Princeton: Princeton University Press, 1993). Explores Nabokov's modernist context.

Fowler, Douglas, *Reading Nabokov* (Ithaca: Cornell University Press, 1974, repr. Washington, DC: University Press of America, 1982).

Frank, Joseph, 'The Lectures of Professor Pnin', in his *Through the Russian Prism: Essays on Literature and Culture* (Princeton: Princeton University Press, 1990), 49–53.

Fraysse, Suzanne, '*Look at the Harlequins!* or the Construction of an Autobiography Through the Reader-Writer Relationship', *Cycnos*, 1 (1993), 143–9.

Gibian, George and Parker, Stephen Jan (eds.), *The Achievements of Vladimir Nabokov* (Ithaca: Cornell Center for International Studies, 1984).

Grabes, Herbert, *Fictitious Biographies: Vladimir Nabokov's English Novels* (The Hague and Paris: Mouton, 1977).

Grabes, Herbert, 'The Deconstruction of Autobiography: *Look at the Harlequins!*', *Cycnos*, 1 (1993), 151–8.

Grayson, Jane, *Nabokov Translated: A Comparison of Nabokov's Russian and English Prose* (Oxford: Oxford University Press, 1977).

Green, Geoffrey, *Freud and Nabokov* (Lincoln: University of Nebraska Press, 1988).

Greenleaf, Monika, 'Fathers, Sons and Impostors: Pushkin's Trace in *The Gift*', *Slavic Review*, 53 (1994), 140–58.

Gregory, Robert, 'Porpoise-iveness Without Porpoise: Why Nabokov Called James a Fish', *The Henry James Review*, 6/1 (1984), 52–9.

Hughes, Robert P., 'Nabokov Reading Pasternak', in Lazar Fleishman (ed.), *Boris Pasternak and His Times* (Berkeley: Berkeley Slavic Specialties, 1989), 153–70.

Hyde, G. M., *Vladimir Nabokov: America's Russian Novelist* (London: Marion Boyars, 1977).

Johnson, D. Barton, 'Belyj and Nabokov: A Comparative Overview', *Russian Literature*, 9 (1981), 379–402.

Johnson, D. Barton, *Worlds in Regression: Some Novels of Vladimir Nabokov* (Ann Arbor: Ardis, 1985). Fundamental work of textual analysis.

Karlinsky, Simon, 'Vladimir Nabokov's Novel *Dar* as a Work of Literary Criticism', *Slavic and East European Journal*, 7 (1963), 284–90.

Levin, Iu. I, 'Ob osobennostiakh povestvovatel'noi struktury i obraznogo stroia romana V. Nabokova *Dar*', *Russian Literature*, 9 (1981), 191–229.

Lodge, David, 'What Kind of Fiction Did Nabokov Write? A Practitioner's View', in his *The Practice of Writing: Essays, Lectures, Reviews and a Diary* (Harmondsworth: Penguin, 1997), 150–69.

McGinn, Colin, 'The Moral Case for *Lolita*', *TLS* (August 29 1997), 14.

Maddox, Lucy, *Nabokov's Novels in English* (Athens: University of Georgia Press, London: Croom Helm, 1983).

Mason, Bobbie Ann, *Nabokov's Garden: A Guide to 'Ada'* (Ann Arbor, Ardis, 1974).

Meyer, Priscilla, *Find What the Sailor Has Hidden: Vladimir Nabokov's 'Pale Fire'* (Middletown, Conn.: Wesleyan University Press, 1988).

Meyer, Priscilla, 'Nabokov's Biographers, Annotators, and Interpreters', *Modern Philology* (1994), 326–38.

Meyer, Priscilla, and Hoffman, Jeff, 'Infinite Reflections in Nabokov's *Pale Fire*: The Danish Connection (Hans Andersen and Isak Dinesen)', *Russian Literature*, 41 (1997), 197–221.

Motte, Warren, 'Authoritarian Nabokov', in his *Playtexts: Ludics in Contemporary Literature* (Lincoln and London: University of Nebraska Press, 1995), 69–90.

Murliachik, A. S., *Russkaia proza Vladimira Nabokova* (Moscow, 1997).

Nakhimovsky, A. and Paperno, S., *An English–Russian Dictionary of Nabokov's 'Lolita'* (Ann Arbor, Ardis: 1982).

Naumann, Marina Turkevich, *Blue Evenings in Berlin: Nabokov's Short*

Stories of the 1920s (New York: New York University Press, 1978).

Naumann, Marina Turkevich, 'Nabokov and Pushkin's Tuning Fork', *Russian Literature*, 29 (1991), 229–42.

Nicol, Charles and Barabtarlo, Gennady (eds.), *A Small Alpine Form: Studies in Nabokov's Short Fiction* (New York: Garland, 1993).

Olsen, Lance, *Lolita: A Janus Text* (New York: Twayne, 1995).

Page, Norman (ed.), *Nabokov: The Critical Heritage* (London: Routledge and Kegan Paul, 1982). Compilation of original reviews.

Paperno, Irina, 'How Nabokov's *Gift* is Made', *Stanford Slavic Studies*, 4/2 (1992), 295–322.

Parker, Stephen Jan, *Understanding Vladimir Nabokov* (Columbia, SC: University of South Carolina Press, 1987).

Pifer, Ellen, *Nabokov and the Novel* (Cambridge, Mass.: Harvard University Press, 1980).

Pifer, Ellen, 'Shades of Love: Nabokov's Intimations of Immortality', *The Kenyon Review*, 11/2 (1989), 75–86.

Pilling, John, 'A Tremulous Prism: Nabokov's *Speak, Memory*', in Jane Gary Harris (ed.), *Autobiographical Statements in Twentieth-Century Russian Literature* (Princeton: Princeton University Press, 1990), 154–71.

Proffer, Carl R., *Keys to Lolita* (Bloomington, Ind.: Indiana University Press, 1968).

Proffer, Ellendea (ed.), *Vladimir Nabokov: A Pictorial Biography* (Ann Arbor: Ardis, 1991).

Quennell, Peter (ed.), *Vladimir Nabokov: A Tribute* (London: Weidenfeld and Nicolson, 1979). Useful miscellany of materials.

Rampton, David, *Vladimir Nabokov: A Critical Study of the Novels* (Cambridge: Cambridge University Press, 1984).

Rampton, David, *Vladimir Nabokov* (Basingstoke and London: Macmillan, 1993).

Rivers, J. E. and Nicol, Charles (eds), *Nabokov's Fifth Arc: Nabokov and Others on His Life's Work* (Austin: University of Texas Press, 1982). A useful collection.

Ronen, Irena and Omry, ' "Diabolically Evocative": An Inquiry into the Meaning of Metaphor', *Slavica Hierosolymitana*, 5–6 (1981), 371–86.

Roth, Phyllis A. (ed.), *Critical Essays on Vladimir Nabokov* (Boston: G. K. Hall, 1984).

Rowe, W. W., *Nabokov's Spectral Dimension* (Ann Arbor: Ardis, 1981).

Saputelli, Linda Nadine, 'The Long-Drawn Sunset of Fialta', in Julian W. Connolly and Sonia I. Ketchian (eds.), *Studies in Russian Literature in Honor of Vsevolod Setchkarev* (Columbus, Ohio: Slavica Publishers, 1986), 233–42.

Senderovich, Savelii and Shvarts, Elena, 'Verbnaia shtuchka: Nabokov i populiarnaia kul'tura', *Novoe literaturnoe obozrenie*, 24 (1997), 93–110; and 26 (1997), 201–22.

Shapiro, Gavriel, *Delicate Markers: Subtexts in Vladimir Nabokov's 'Invitation to a Beheading'* (New York, Peter Lang, 1998).

Sharpe, Tony, *Vladimir Nabokov* (London: Edward Arnold, 1991).

Shrayer, Maxim D., 'Mapping Narrative Space in Nabokov's Short Fiction', *The Slavonic and East European Review*, 75 (1997a), 624–41.

Shrayer, Maxim D., 'Decoding Vladimir Nabokov's "The Return of Chorb"', *Russian Language Journal*, 51/168–170 (1997b), 177–202.

Shrayer, Maxim D., 'Nabokov's Textobiography', *The Modern Language Review*, 94/1 (1999), 132–49.

Stegner, Page, *Escape into Aesthetics: The Art of Vladimir Nabokov* (New York: Dial, 1966; London: Eyre and Spottiswoode, 1967).

Swanson, Roy Arthur, Nabokov's *Ada* as Science Fiction', *Science-Fiction Studies*, 2/1 (March 1975), 76–88.

Tamir-Ghez, Nomi, 'Rhetorical Manipulation in Nabokov's *Lolita*', in Andrej Kodjak *et al.* (eds.), *The Structural Analysis of Narrative Texts* (Columbus, Oh.: Slavica, 1980), 172–95; rev. version in Roth (1984).

Tammi, Pekka, *Problems of Nabokov's Poetics: A Narratological Analysis* (Helsinki: Suomalainen Tiedeakaternia, 1985). Important examination of narratological method.

Toker, Leona, *Nabokov: The Mystery of Literary Structures* (Ithaca: Cornell University Press, 1989).

Torgovnick, Marianna, 'Nabokov and his Successors: *Pale Fire* as a Fable for Critics in the Seventies and Eighties', *Style*, 20/1 (1986), 22–41.

V. V. Nabokov: pro et contra Lichnost' i tvorchestvo Vladimira Nabokova v otsenke russkikh i zarubezhnykh myslitelei i issledovatelei. Antologiia, [ed. by B. Averin *et al.*] (St Petersburg, 1997). Vast compilation (in Russian) of Western and Russian scholarship.

Waite, Sarah Tiffany, 'On the Linear Structure of Nabokov's *Dar*: Three Keys, Six Chapters', *Slavic and East European Journal*, 39 (1995), 54–72.

Wood, Michael, *The Magician's Doubts: Nabokov and the Risks of Fiction* (London: Chatto and Windus, 1994; Princeton: Princeton University Press, 1995).

Zinik, Zinovy, 'The self-sufficiency of style', *TLS* (August 2 1996), 21–2.

Bibliography

Field, Andrew, *Nabokov: A Bibliography* (New York: McGraw-Hill, 1973).

Juliar, Michael, *Vladimir Nabokov: A Descriptive Bibliography* (New York: Garland, 1986).

Schuman, Samuel, *Vladimir Nabokov: A Reference Guide* (Boston: G. K. Hall, 1979).

Journals: Special Issues

Modern Fiction Studies, 25/3 (1979), 'Special Issue: Vladimir Nabokov'.

Russian Literature Triquarterly, 24 (1991): 'Nabokov'.
Russian Literature, 43/3 (1998): 'Special Issue: Vladimir Nabokov'.

Nabokov Journals

The Vladimir Nabokov Research Newsletter, 1978–84; subsequently *The Nabokovian*, Lawrence: University of Kansas Press, 1984–.
Nabokov Studies, Los Angeles, Schlacks, subsequently Davidson, NC: Davidson College, 1994–.
Nabokovskii vestnik, St Petersburg, 1998–.

Web Sites

Vladimir Nabokov Forum: NABOKV-L@UCSBVM.UCSB.EDU
ZEMBLA: The Web Site for Vladimir Nabokov, URL:
   http://www.libraries.psu.edu/iasweb/nabokov/nsintro.htm

GENERAL

Studies or books which include sections on, or comments relevant to, Nabokov.

Alexander, Marguerite, *Flights from Realism: Themes and Strategies in Postmodernist British and American Fiction* (London: Edward Arnold, 1990).
Baxter, John, *Stanley Kubrick: A Biography* (London: HarperCollins, 1997).
Beaujour, Elizabeth Klosty, *Alien Tongues: Bilingual Russian Writers of the 'First' Emigration* (Ithaca: Cornell University Press, 1989). A useful chapter on Nabokov.
Berberova, Nina, *The Italics Are Mine: An Autobiography* (New York: Harcourt Brace, 1969). Memoirs of the first emigration.
Brostrom, Kenneth N. (ed.), *Russian Literature and American Critics: In Honor of Deming Brown* (Ann Arbor: Department of Slavic Languages and Literatures, University of Michigan, 1984). Includes essays on Nabokov.
Bruss, Elizabeth, *Autobiographical Acts: The Changing Situation of a Literary Genre* (Baltimore, Johns Hopkins University Press, 1976).
Charney, Maurice, *Sexual Fiction* (London: Methuen, 1981).
Cornwell, Neil, *James Joyce and the Russians* (Basingstoke and London: Macmillan, 1992). Includes an account of Nabokov's relations with Joyce.
Cornwell, Neil (ed.), *Reference Guide to Russian Literature* (London and Chicago: Fitzroy Dearborn, 1998). Includes essays on several of

Nabokov's Russian works.

Dipple, Elizabeth, *The Unresolvable Plot: Reading Contemporary Fiction* (New York and London: Routledge, 1988).

Gardner, Martin, *The Ambidextrous Universe: Mirror Asymmetry and Time-Reversed Worlds.* (2nd rev., updated ed., New York: Charles Scribner's & Sons, 1979).

Genette, Gérard, *Paratexts: Thresholds of Interpretation,* transl. by Jane E. Lewin (Cambridge: Cambridge University Press, 1997; first publ. in French, 1987).

Green, Martin and Swan, John, *The Triumph of Pierrot: The Commedia dell'Arte and the Modern Imagination* (rev. ed., University Park, Pennsylvania: Pennsylvania State University Press, 1993).

Hochman, Baruch, *Character in Literature* (Ithaca and London: Cornell University Press, 1985).

Hutcheon, Linda, *Narcissistic Narrative: The Metafictional Paradox* (New York and London: Methuen, 1984; first publ. 1980).

Kael, Pauline, *I Lost It at the Movies: Film Writings 1954–1965* (New York and London: Marion Boyars, 1994; first publ. 1965).

Kaznina, O., *Russkie v Anglii. Russkaia emigratsiia v kontekste russko-angliiskikh literaturnykh sviazei v pervoi polovine XX veka* (Moscow, 1997). Includes an account of Nabokov in England.

Lachmann, Renate, *Memory and Literature: Intertextuality in Russian Modernism,* transl. by Roy Sellars and Anthony Wall (Minneapolis and London: University of Minnesota Press, 1997; first publ. in German 1990).

McHale, Brian, *Postmodernist Fiction* (New York and London: Methuen, 1987).

McHale, Brian, *Constructing Postmodernism* (London: Routledge, 1992).

Rancour-Laferriere, Daniel (ed.), *Russian Literature and Psychoanalysis* (Amsterdam: John Benjamins, 1989). Includes essays on Nabokov.

Rayfield, Donald (ed.), *The Confessions of Victor X* (London: Caliban, 1984). One source for *Lolita*.

Rorty, Richard, *Contingency, Irony and Solidarity* (Cambridge: Cambridge University Press, 1989). Includes an important essay on Nabokov and ethics.

Steiner, George, *Extraterritorial: Papers on Literature and the Language Revolution* (Harmondsworth: Penguin, 1975, first publ. 1971).

Thibault, Paul J., *Social Semiotics as Praxis: Text, Social Meaning Making, and Nabokov's 'Ada'* (Minneapolis: University of Minnesota Press, 1991). *Ada* is used as a sample text.

Waugh, Patricia, *Metafiction: The Theory and Practice of Self-Conscious Fiction* (London: Methuen, 1984).

Zholkovsky, Alexander, *Text counter Text: Rereadings in Russian Literary History* (Stanford: Stanford University Press, 1994).

Index